The BOYS of Glacier

Michael G. Impero

This book is dedicated to:

SUSIE IMPERO: My Wife and Partner in Everything for 52 Years.

To all of those who helped in writing "The Boys":

Special Thanks

Gerrit Byeman is a special friend who helped so much with this book and the others. Many of the photos in this book were taken by Gerrit. The cover was created by him. He is a great partner for exploring the mountains, as he was trained in mountain ways by his long-time friend, Jerry Bourn.

John Impero, the author's brother, spent hours reviewing the works. He also was great help with the "Boys"and bringing them to life.

Thanks

Doug Hamilton
Chuck Jenkins
Karen Kok
Charlotte Kvistad
John Munroe
Jake Steiner
Ron Nelson
Roy Nelson
Jerry Conger
Don Brown
Frank Bottiger
Pamp Maiers
Todd Warger
Gary Graham
Ralph Graham
Sunshine Printing-Rose Nerad
Whatcom Museum-Jeff Jewel
National Archives and Records
Administration-Patty McNamee
Western Washington University
Archives-Tony Kurtz
Washington State Archives, NW
Regional Branch-Allison Costanza
Western Washington University
CPNWS-Ruth Steele
Bellingham Library

Author Notes

1. Stuart (Stu) and Elizabeth McKenzie were totally fictitious characters. Any connections to anyone by these two names is strictly coincidental.
2. All of the "Boys" named in this book were real people. Only a few of the named people remain alive. All of the stories are as told by friends and family of the individuals. In some cases, yes, the author did modify the stories.
3. Whatcom County of Washington does exist.
4. Graham's in Glacier remains to exist after 100 years.

Table of Contents

Table of Contents

continued

Introduction

TOWN of GLACIER

Scale 200 feet to one inch.

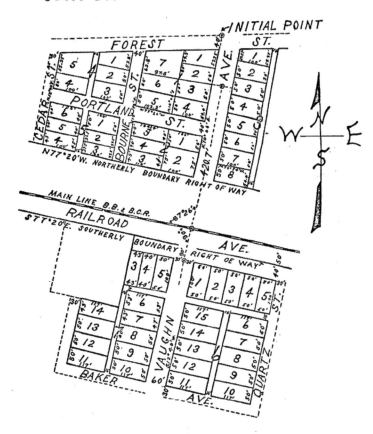

This plat lies N.E. corner of the N.W. quarter
of the N.E. quarter and the N.W. corner of
Lot 2 of Section 7, Twp. 39 N., R. 7 E., W. M.

VOLUME 6, PAGE 2.   W. F. E.

ORIGINAL VAUGHN PLAT OF GLACIER,
WHATCOM COUNTY, WASHINGTON
(Western Washington University-Washington State Archives)

MILLER'S ADDITION to GLACIER

Scale 100 feet to one inch

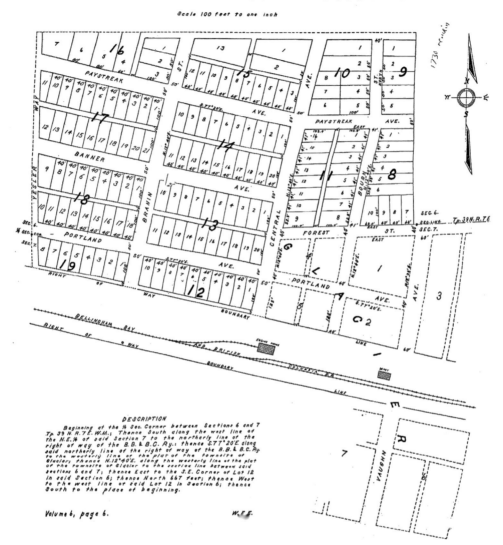

DESCRIPTION

Beginning at the ¼ Sec. Corner between Sections 6 and 7 Tp. 39 N. R. 7 E. W.M.; Thence South along the west line of the N.E.¼ of said Section 7 to the northerly line of the right of way of the B.B.& B.C. Ry.; thence S.77°20'E. along said northerly line of the right of way of the B.B.& B.C. Ry. to the westerly line of the plat of the townsite of Glacier; thence N.12°40'E. along the westerly line of the plat of the townsite of Glacier to the section line between said sections 6 and 7; thence East to the S.E. Corner of Lot 12 in said Section 6; thence North 667 feet; thence West to the west line of said Lot 12 in Section 6; thence South to the place of beginning.

Volume 6, page 6.   W.F.E.

MILLER ADDITION TO GLACIER
(Western Washington University-Washington State Archives)

TOWN OF GLACIER ABOUT 1906 OR 1907
The original platting of the town of Glacier occupied on September 7, 1909 by
Jennie Vaughan and the Miller's Addition to Glacier was platted on May 12,
1910. The Miller's Addition is located all to the north and west of the 1909
plat. The original plat was located on both sides of B.B. & B.C. Railroad.
Portland Street in the original plat was to become the Mt. Baker Highway.
(A) B.B. & B.C. Glacier Depot, (B) Depot Storage Platform, (C) Mountain
Home Hotel, (D) Haggard & Bottiger Store, (E) Hinton Store–later to become
Graham's, (F) Glacier City Hall, (G) McKenzie Livery Stable, (H) Hotel
Glacier, (I) U.S. Forest Ranger Residence. (J. Steiner)

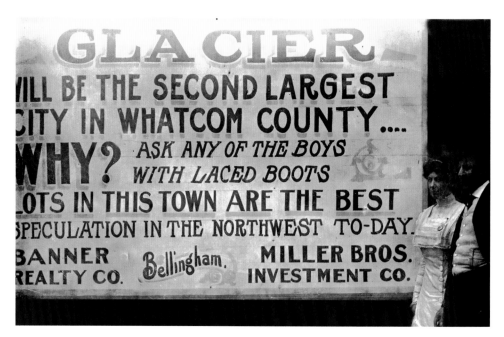

**MILLER BROS. CREATED THE MILLER PLAT
ADDITION TO GLACIER IN 1909**
The Miller Bros. Investment Co. had big plans for Glacier in 1910.
(W. Gannaway)

MOUNTAIN HOME HOTEL, GLACIER'S FIRST HOTEL
(Whatcom Museum, Bellingham, WA)

WHIP AND BLANCHE JACOBS

The Jacobs' constructed the first real hotel in Glacier, the Mountain Home Hotel. Whip was district manager for the Bellingham Bay & British Columbia Railroad and he was stationed in Glacier. Seeing the need, he and his wife built the hotel. The hotel was of lower quality and was used mainly for the working class; railroad workers, loggers, and miners. The hotel could handle about forty guests. The building only stood for a short time as when half the town burned, it, along with the train depot and others, were destroyed. Blanche ran the facility and was respected by all. (M. Impero)

GLACIER POST OFFICE

Glacier, over the years, has had many locations for the post office. In the beginning, Glacier was named Cornell and that name was used for a few years. However, when they formed their first post office the name was too similar to another in the state, so a name change was required. The name chosen was Glacier. George Gray became the first Postmaster in 1903. However, the first post office in the area was at Excelsior. (Norman Huber Collection, Whatcom Museum, Bellingham, WA)

Introduction
The Bucket List

Well, here I—Stuart McKenzie—have returned to Bellingham, Washington—the state of Washington. I traveled the distance from Boston to return to a small town in the northwest corner of the state. Tomorrow is my seventy-fifth year of life and is the day I begin to perform the items I placed on my bucket list. It took me six months to complete the final draft of the five items on the list and each time I wrote them down, this item here in Washington always came to be number one. My wife of fifty years has remained in Boston; she doesn't comprehend this trip to be so important on anyone's list. She has heard me talk about it so much, both to her and to others, that she knows it as well as I do. She also thinks that this region of the country is totally uncivilized, and she could lose her scalp out here. No, I'm not here to see the killer whales so famous in Puget Sound, and I am too old to make an ascent of Mt. Baker. However, in my youth, climbing Mt. Baker was high on my list.

The number one entry on my bucket list is to revisit the small settlement of Glacier, here in Whatcom County. My parents and I had lived in Seattle where my father ran a successful business. He was killed suddenly in an automobile accident, leaving my mother and me alone, struggling to make it on our own. The three of us had been a very close family, but upon his death we had a dreadful time of it for the next two years. Without any other male

figures in my life, as I was without any uncles or grandfathers, my mother decided that we needed to relocate to a place with real outdoorsmen and good mountain air.

For many years our family had received a Christmas card from an Amos Zimmer who lived in Glacier, Washington. Amos was a distant uncle on my father's side. He had written of the beauty of the mountains and had sent numerous photos of the area. This region was the area around Glacier. What we did not know is that Amos had passed away since his last Christmas card.

Mother informed me that with dad's death she had lost all of our savings and that she was required to seek employment. She fabricated the story of the loss of the family savings to get the point across. We relocated to Glacier from Seattle when I was twelve years old; a pimply-faced, skinny, immature kid. Mother applied for and got a job working as a cook in a little store/restaurant/bar named Graham's in Glacier. Earl Graham owned the place and had a small cabin that my mother and I moved into. Mother didn't really have to do this, but felt that she had to get me out of Seattle's lifestyle.

Following graduation from Mt. Baker High School, I joined the army the next October. I lived in Glacier for six years and left there a man. I did my time in the service and then went on to college with the help of the GI bill. After receiving a history degree, along with my masters and a doctorate, from three or four different universities, I taught history my whole working career, teaching at one of Boston's grand universities. The day I joined the service my mother returned back to our house in Seattle.

Since the day I left Glacier, I had not returned nor had I kept in contact with any of the people; then I decided to make a trip back…

As my airplane approaches Bellingham, I notice quickly that it is now a major city in the Northwest. In the past it had a huge paper mill, and Bellingham Bay was commonly quite full of floating logs. These logs would be used in the pulp mill or shipped by water to other mills in the area. I had gotten a firsthand look at the pulp mill and the floating logs as many times I had ridden to Bellingham in logging trucks, sometimes with a driver named Six-Pack Ernie.

As we approach Bellingham Bay, I suddenly realize that there are no floating logs in the bay and that the majority of the huge paper mill has been removed. There is no huge smokestack that was a common sight when approaching Bellingham. What could've happened to this large industry, as this was one of the major employers in the area?

In my rental car, I head out to revisit Glacier. It's a bright August morning; perfect for my trip. After getting directions from the desk clerk on how to locate the Mt. Baker Highway, I'm off. The highway is now numbered as 542 but at one point it was State Highway Number One. As I pass over the freeway, which wasn't there last time, I look to the left to see old Jack's Chain Saw Shop, complete with three or four

TYPICAL LOGGING TRUCK
Each day hundreds of these trucks made the trip from the mountains to local mills or the large mill in Bellingham. The timber was harvested from private, state, and federal lands. At one point in Whatcom County history, the forest industry was the largest employer. (F. Bottiger)

old beat up logger's pickups parked in front, but no, the site is now a Burger King.

Heading out of town down Y Road hill, I should see Bob Curtis' (sometimes named Jessie James) Truck Repair Shop on the right, but I notice that it is closed up. Where are all the logging trucks on the Y Road hill? Years ago, there would have been over four hundred loads of logs delivered each day to Bellingham down this road. In those days, it would be common that a whole procession of these trucks would be slowly moving up this hill, at maybe ten miles per hour. Always in front of the line would be an old army truck made into a logging truck with no power, or Six Pack Ernie's truck, would be in the lead.

Suddenly, there is that mountain —Mt. Baker—in full view. What a magnificent sight! But, along with that beautiful sight come memories… Oh god, what was her name? Oh yeah, Alice… Alice James. She could have been a grandmother by now, and lived a full life, except for what happened that one day. One of the worst days in my life was up on that mountain.

Unexpectedly I come upon roundabouts in two spots. The old steel Nugent's Bridge is gone, having been replaced with a modern, concrete one. Over-height logging trucks were always damaging the end, overhead portal braces of the old bridge. Otto's Repair Shop is still there but it has a different name. The old Kendall School is long gone; now a library rests in its spot. The Kendall Store, with its submarine sandwiches, appears totally changed now.

The old Haggard Store in Maple Falls is lost to history, replaced with something new. The gas station with the "Billy Goat" wreckers has also disappeared. Across Boulder Creek, I would be at the CCC (Civil Conservation Corp) Camp, which housed a couple hundred men. Now it's a church camp, and all the CCC Camp buildings are removed. The old, steel Warnick Bridge has remained as it was, steel, but the railroad bridge is gone. The Miller Shingle Mill is nothing but a stand of cottonwood trees.

From here on, I slow down and pass the Bottiger Farm. I recall back in my days of being a cowboy, when these fields were full of the Bottiger cows, which were a total mixed breed. They always appeared to be especially skinny. I see that the house and barn with all the out buildings have not been here for decades. Next, the old school site comes into view. Later it became a restaurant, but it is also gone.

I park near Grahams' and looking diagonally across the street, I see only remains of a burned down Mt. Baker Inn. Only a few walls are standing of what was probably the second or third inn. I walk the whole town, seeing the old depot, train foreman's house, and town hall. Pamp Bottiger's house and equipment shop remain with a different name on the mailbox. I walk up the road, crossing where the railroad tracks had been, looking for Jumbo Bill's cabin—not a trace remains, only blackberry bushes eight feet tall. Glacier has a fresh new fire station; probably the first, and a gourmet Italian restaurant.

Oh yes; now I must find the cabin that mother and I resided in. It was located up above the railroad tracks near

**TWO OF THE BOYS–MINER BILL ON LEFT AND JAKE STEINER
HAVING A COLD ONE**

**Jake Steiner, born in Glacier, lived his entire life on his father's homestead.
He was not eligible for World War II due to the fact that he was injured in a
mechanical accident when he was six years old. The service that he did provide
in the war was with Frank Bottiger, they served as Japanese Airplane spotter's
in the Glacier area. Jake was employed as a timber cutter his whole working
career and also farmed the homestead. Miner Bill came to Glacier in search of
copper and silver and after a decade or two, he moved on. (J. Steiner)**

the area of Jumbo Bill's. My mother
and I lived in this cabin for six years,
and it was certainly an education; far
cry from my condo in Boston, or even
our house in Seattle. We did have
running water and even had hot water
when the wood stove was in use.

Our cabin was the most rustic
structure that you could imagine. It was
very small, with two small bedrooms,
one bathroom, and a kitchen area. The
outside of the structure was sheeted
with lumber and the interior walls

and ceiling was completed with finish
lumber. The floor was sheeted with
rough lumber, and then covered with
linoleum. When a strong windstorm
was in the area, a breeze would blow
right through the house. Thank god, the
wind blew very seldom in Glacier.

One summer, with daytime
temperatures extremely high, we
detected that wild blackberries were
growing through the cracks in the wall
and into my bedroom. We decided to
let them grow and later in September we

GRAHAM'S STORE, RESTAURANT, AND BAR 2012
Same location and building after over a hundred years and the benches line the wall in front of the windows. The Graham Family owned this establishment since 1932. Today, the facility caters to the local people, tourists, and winter sports. (G. Byeman)

had enough for a wild blackberry pie. When we first moved into the cabin, I could not believe that my mother was allowing us to live in such a place. But after a couple of weeks, we were both happy in this new environment and did not miss our modern house in Seattle at all.

We only ate one meal—breakfast—in the cabin, and the other two were down at Graham's. The cabin was just a short distance from Graham's, and we would just walk back and forth. I know precisely where it should be, but I'm not sure that I am in the right location. One of the problems when you reach my age is that sometimes your memory skips a gear or two, but I just can't find the cabin. No, there's not a trace of it. I guess that's not surprising when you realize it was decomposing when we left.

As I continue my walk, I come to the area where I should find the intake to the Glacier Water System. Along with other things, the Grahams owned the

water system. This included the water intake and the wood pipes throughout the town. The Grahams maintained the water and charged $.50 per month for each user. The water intake was a bathtub up in the creek with a screen on the top. It was my job to go up weekly and take away all the debris, which came down the creek and plugged the screen. The whole town of Glacier, on different occasions, would be without water and I'd go up, and within minutes have the system working once more. I can remember a couple of times that water customers came into Grahams and reported small trout in their kitchen sink.

With fewer houses than in my teen years, everything seems to be closed-in and smaller. I start to wonder if I should have listened to my wife about this being number one on my bucket list.

I walk into Graham's and as I scan about slowly, it all starts to come back. All of a sudden I can smell the tobacco

**GARY AND PARKER GRAHAM–THE OWNERS OF
GRAHAM'S IN GLACIER**

**The Graham family purchased the building and business when the previous
owner lost the building to a gambling debt. Today it remains in the family
with two brothers, Gary and Parker, as owners and operators. (Jack Carver
Photo-Whatcom Museum, Bellingham, WA)**

aroma that used to hang in the space above the bar and that sweet smell of chewing tobacco is still there. The odor of all of the alcohol that had soaked into the floor for almost 100 years gives the room a bit of an identifiable odor.

The huge cobwebs still exist up in the corners of the ceiling and on the light fixtures. The potbellied stove is still in the same place, but the large cushioned chairs that surround it have disappeared. That wood floor is still the same, having survived being chewed up by years of logger's cork boots. In some areas, I can see that the building has been modernized, particularly the kitchen area where my mother slaved

for six years. The post office equipment and all of the grocery products have been removed. The current use of the building is strictly a bar and restaurant now.

I turn to look to the back door. I can't believe I saw Jerry riding his horse through that door. As I turn to look out at the front windows, I can still see Jerry throwing the rock, with him attached, right through the window.

Oh, by god, the bar and the barstools are exactly the same! That bar came around the Cape by sailing ship and arrived in Seattle, but ultimately ended up here. It has more character than any other that I've seen in my 75 years. It

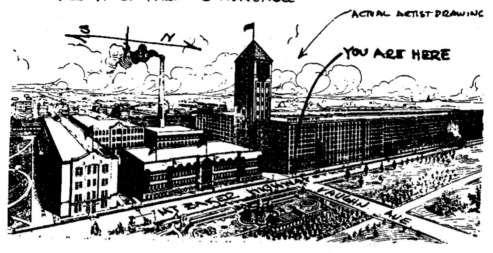

GRAHAMS RESTAURANT
IN THE HEART OF DOWN TOWN
GLACIER WASHINGTON U.S.A,
"PLENTY OF PARKING AVAILABLE"

ACTUAL ARTIST DRAWING

YOU ARE HERE

ONE FORM OF GRAHAM'S ADVERTISING

The Graham Brothers were very creative in their advertising and as one can see they have the two streets that intersect in front of Grahams' identified, the Mt. Baker Highway (originally Portland Street) and Vaughn Avenue. The two brothers, a decade or so ago, one clear day decided it would be nice to eat dinner that evening in the Church Mountain Meadows. After spending most of the day in preparation, they hired a helicopter that was flying out of Glacier, and the helicopter ferried everything to the top of the mountain. Included were tables, chairs, dishes, silverware and white napkins. All the guests eating the dinner were dressed in suits and dresses and were hauled to the mountaintop. After dinner, wine, and a beautiful sunset, the whole party and all the provisions were flown back to Glacier. (T. Warger)

GRAHAM'S BAR 2013
The bar in Graham's is possibly worth more than the rest of the building. Rumor has it that the bar came around the Cape in a sailing ship and then served in Seattle for many years. It then came to Glacier on the train and has remained in the same spot since its placement. (G. Byeman)

looks a little worse for wear, but it's the same one. What a piece of art.

I find a table in the back corner, sit down, and continue to remember. In a few minutes, a cute young girl, about one third my age arrives to get my order. I ask her if by any chance the Graham family is the owner and if any of the family work here. She answers, "Yes," and points to where her boss is standing at the end of the bar. I ask if I can speak to him, and she goes to get him. Gary arrives at the table. I introduce myself and a four-hour conversation follows.

Gary is a friendly young man. He tells me of his life as an engineer at Boeing and his move back to Glacier. His brother Parker and he now operate

the store/restaurant. He is very knowledgeable about all the local people at this time and tells loads of stories about them. Gary is certainly different than his grandfather. His grandfather, at times, could be very quiet, reserved, and lost in thought. At other times, he would take the time and describe to me countless events around Glacier. I remember that his wife was a lovely lady and seemed to be somewhat in charge most of the time.

After drinking a couple of beers and consuming a great hamburger—on the house—we had covered almost all the history of the last 50 years of Glacier; things like how the forest service had changed, all of the recreational development that had taken place east

GLACIER TOWNSHIP CEMETERY
The Glacier Cemetery is one of the most beautiful cemeteries in the area. It is nested back in the evergreens and one can see all of the natural ferns and moss that enhance the area. (G. Byeman)

of Glacier, about the schools, some of the families, and the fact that Glacier now has a gourmet Italian restaurant. At this rate, I decide that it is time to ask Gary all about the boys.

Just as I was about to ask the most important question of all—about the boys—Gary jumps up and announces that he is late for a business meeting in Bellingham. He excuses himself, we shake hands, and say goodbye.

After drinking the last of my beer and upon getting up, I remember that when I entered Graham's, I did see three benches out front. I must go take a look. In approaching the first two, I recognize them to be brand-new, cast iron benches; the kind that you see all over, but upon looking closer, I realize that the bench on the far end is an original. The shock of joy that hits me

is overwhelming as I go to the bench.

As I sit down, I can't believe that this could be the same bench. There must be some way that I can prove it to myself. Thinking for a second, I start to search. And yes, here it is. I run my hand over the initials. After all these years, it is still legible: S.M. + S.M. Sue Miller was my first girlfriend here in Glacier in my junior year of high school. Looking at those initials, after all these years, I must admit it is a great carving job! Pamp Bottiger had given me a beautiful jackknife for helping his son, Frankie, search for his cow. Believe it or not, I still have that knife.

When I first arrived in Glacier with my mother, she set up boundaries for the first week. One of those was that the store, our cabin, and out front by the benches, was as far as I could go.

Within a few weeks, she expanded my boundaries, and within six months I had the run of the whole town.

I sit on the bench with my memories for the rest of the afternoon and when total darkness is upon Glacier, I realize that I have dozed off. I realize that Graham's has closed for the day and the town is almost dark. At one point, I can almost hear The Boys in deep debate early in the afternoon or in an argument about some important issue in their world. Frank Bottiger and Jumbo Bill are the voices that stand out.

As I stand up, I detect an elderly gentleman approaching me on the boardwalk. He obviously had come to the post office to collect his mail. As he approaches my location, I notice how erect he is walking. I say, "Good evening, how are you doing tonight?"

In a very solid voice he replies, "Very good; a fine evening."

I decide to ask him a question. "If you don't mind me asking, how long have you lived here in the Glacier area?"

The man replies, "I've lived here all my life, just down the road a bit, and that would make it 92 years."

All of a sudden a light bulb goes on in my head and I ask, "If you don't mind me asking, what would be your name?"

I wait for the answer and slowly the man responds, "My name is Jake Steiner." I couldn't believe what I just heard, for this man was one of the original "Boys!"

"Mr. Steiner, I can't expect you to remember me, but my name is Stuart McKenzie, Stu for short. I resided here for six years as my mother was a cook at Graham's," I say.

Jake stands back, takes a serious look at me and replies, "Can't say that I do."

I don't give up and fire another question, "Could you make time to tell me what became of all the boys—the Bottigers, the Bourns, Jumbo Bill, and the Grahams?"

Jake pauses for a minute and says, "I'd be happy to talk with you, but I've got to get home now for I can't drive so well after dark."

I ask, "How about meeting me here tomorrow at four o'clock and you can fill me in?"

Jake takes a very serious look at me and excitedly replies, "I do remember you; you were that runt of a little kid that hung around this bench all the time. You bet; I'll be here at four o'clock tomorrow afternoon. Good night."

I can't believe my good luck, and I jump up with joy as much as a 75-year-old man can jump. As I leave town and head to Bellingham, I know that I will positively return tomorrow. That trip will take me to the Glacier Cemetery, Twin Lakes, with a hike to the Lone Jack Mine, and an outing to Jerry's cabin. The last thing of the day will be the highlight, catching up with Jake.

On my seventy-fifth year and one day of life, I return my first rental sedan and leave with an SUV. My life in Boston doesn't require that I know what an SUV is. As I'm driving out the Mt. Baker Highway for the second time, I notice additional changes to buildings, among other things. As I approach Glacier, I see that there is a speed limit sign; in my youth I don't remember any sign on the highway; it must have been there. If the speed limit sign had been there when I was a young kid, it would have been totally shot full of holes.

20

I drive through town and stop at the Mt. Baker National Forest Ranger Station. "Wait, " I think, "what's this?" The sign reads, "Mt. Baker-Snoqualmie National Forest." Right away I see that it is now named the Visitors Center. I see no Forest Service Ranger pickup, and no logging trucks parked across the road at the truck scaling platform. I enter the station and find three young, cute women in their ranger uniforms. I ask where the men forest rangers are, and they tell me that there are no real rangers. This ranger station is only used in the summer. I ask about the logging, and they answer that there is no logging in this district.

Next, they give me directions to the Glacier Cemetery. I inquire of the condition of the Twin Lakes Road and the trail from Gold Run Pass Trail to the lakes. I am told that the road goes all the way to the lakes. I cannot believe this information but am delighted to hear it. I ask how to find Jerry's cabin and they tell me the shocking news that it is gone, burned down.

"How could you allow that to happen? Were you not the protector of the property of the forest?" I ask, but got no answer.

The original road to the cemetery is somewhat grown over but could be followed. The main entry on the north side today is from a housing development. The cemetery has not changed a great deal from years ago, and I am surprised that some names I expected to find were not there. Upon looking further I find that all the graves are arranged in a circle. I realize that in years past people would have arrived by horse drawn wagons and they would make a circle turn.

"Where is Jerry Bourn? He must be here. Here is his dad. Why would Jerry not be buried here?" I ask myself. In disbelief, I head back to my car—if I can find it.

Starting up the Twin Lakes Road, I see a sign that tells me that a mining company is using this road. How exciting that is! "Could it be the old Jack?" I ask myself.

A couple of miles beyond, I come upon an ore truck that is stopped along side the road as the driver allows his brakes to cool. I stop for a little information and ask if they are again mining the Jack. Old Jerry didn't get it all. They were mining it again! I am told that a small three to four man crew operated the mine on a seasonal basis. I had to get going for a look.

Upon arriving at the Gold Run Pass Trail, I count thirty-three cars parked at the trailhead and this was mid-week! I continue up and the road gets steeper, with switchbacks. The SUV is doing fine; probably should have put the four wheel in gear, but wasn't sure how to do it.

Upon arriving at the lakes, I again am shocked by all the cars in the parking lot. Adults, kids, and dogs wander all over. When Jerry Bourn and I visited this beautiful spot, there was no one here except the two fishermen out in the middle of the lake on a makeshift raft. I park alongside the other cars and sit on a rock on the hillside, viewing the lakes. As I concentrate and close my eyes to almost everything, my thoughts return to the day with Jerry. The beauty of those two lakes was unmatched in my lifetime with anything else.

I walk past the lakes and take the same trail that Jerry and I had used.

Being in the high meadows, nothing has changed in all these years. I reach the point as I had with Jerry and look down into Lulu Gulch. The Packrat Hilton and the ore building are completely gone; nothing but trees and more trees. I see the mining operation, but you must look hard because it is such a low impact operation. I head back to the lakes and have one last look. I want the lakes to be as they had been, but I know that that can't be. Driving down in the switchbacks I smell a burning odor. It smells just like the ore truck. I should stop and let my vehicle cool down; I'm in no hurry.

I park at the end of Jerry's driveway and slowly walk in. As I near the cabin site, I can smell the coffee and stew on the stove. The cabin is totally gone; only some scraps of sheet metal remain. I head to Jerry's Pond and the waterwheel is also gone without a trace. As I come to the pond, the dam is no longer there. I can't make out where it was and the pond is nothing but marshy land now. Back at the cabin site, the field out in front where Jerry kept the dogs has completely grown back to trees. That beautiful site from Jerry's front window, the view of the north face of Mt. Shuksan, is completely blocked with second-growth fir trees. That view was unmatched in my lifetime. I spend another half an hour and head down the road. The old memories are the best.

Jake and I both arrive at exactly 4 o'clock. He is driving a 20-year-old small farm pickup with a great big black dog in the back. As I meet him, I ask, "Would you like to go inside, have a cold beer, and discuss the 'Boys'?"

He replies, "No, I gave up drinking years ago, and I would rather sit out here in the sun."

We first discuss where I had gone today and the changes that I had seen. As I am telling him of each location that I visited, he slowly shakes his head. "It's a shame, it's just a damn shame that things have to change. They call it progress! All my friends here in Glacier are gone now and I can honestly say that I am ready to move on, too."

He began to fill me in on the Boys of Glacier. "Well, I can't really recall the sequence of the boys kicking off, so I'll just start with old Frank Bottiger. As you can imagine Frank, as time went on, was really abusing his body. You may not recall, but old Frank was a magnificent looking young man. Well, son Leck got in the habit of driving to Detroit and picking up a new Oldsmobile every year. This one particular year, he took his dad along. The intent was to drop old Frank off at relatives in one of those Midwestern states and pick him up on the return trip. Everything went as planned. After getting his new car, he picked up Frank and the two of them headed for home. At some point on the return trip, Leck realized that his dad had died. He left him in the front seat, drove across four state lines, and continued to buy wine for both Frank and himself. Needless to say, Leck drank both of their shares. Frank is buried in the Glacier cemetery."

Jake continued, "Now, Pamp Bottiger's death was an odd one. Pamp and brother Leck were logging up Glacier Creek Road. On this particular day they were cutting and bucking timber. Pamp was cutting down a big, ugly maple tree. On its way down, it struck a second tree and a large branch

THE LAST OF THE BOYS
With the passing of these four men, all of the original Boys of Glacier are gone.
(J. Steiner)

fell and struck Pamp on the head. Pamp, along with Leck, walked to their pickup and headed to Bellingham. In route, they stopped, once or twice, for beer.

Pamp walked into the hospital to the emergency room, sat down, and then was told to lie down. The moment he laid down, he became unconscious and lived in that condition for 35 years. He just died a few years ago.

"Leck had a weird death also. After Pamp's death, he and his nephew, young Pamp, went to Moses Lake. After a night of heavy drinking, he and a second man returned to his trailer house for a few more drinks. This man severely beat Leck and stole everything of value. Leck died within a few days.

"Jumbo Bill and Lars Fry both just died.

"Well, that's probably about all I remember," Jake recalled.

Having listened intently I ask, "What about Jerry Bourn?"

Jake quickly started in again. "Oh yes, Jerry my good friend. Jerry was killed in a car wreck when the car he was in went off the road at the top of Power Plant Hill. It was in the middle of winter and the roads above Glacier were extremely icy. A good samaritan in Glacier was giving Jerry a ride home and the car went off the road and hit a large tree. If the tree had not been there, the car would have plunged another 200 feet into the river. It was in 1980."

After hearing the story from Jake of Jerry's death, we both fell silent. I thought about how this man died in a car wreck and not in the mountains. It was unbelievable. You would have thought that he would have been buried with part of the ceiling of the stope from the Lone Jack Mine collapsed on him or that he would have drowned when Silesia Creek was in flood stage… or he could have been shot by the owners of mines or the placer claims that he had been high grading for years. Maybe the mountains just couldn't kill him.

"What about the Earl and Mrs. Earl?" I asked. I always called her Mrs. Earl.

Jake's answer was brief, "Well, I don't remember when, but the two of them moved back to Bellingham, retired, and died there."

Jake and I continued to talk for another half an hour. All of a sudden it seemed like we had run out of things to say, so I decided that it was time for me to leave. I thanked him and excused myself by saying that I had to get back to Bellingham and prepare for an early morning flight. We said goodbye knowing that we would never see each other again. As Jake walked away and approached his beat up old pickup, I could see his dog in the back jumping up and down with excitement.

As I slowly drive out of Glacier for the second and final time, I turn to look over my shoulder for one last look as I say my goodbyes. Tomorrow, I will head back to my current world, not this world of my childhood, but I am ready to reassure my wife that Glacier was truly number one on my bucket list.

Year Number One

GRAHAM'S WOOD BENCH

Within 24 hours of their arrival in Glacier, Stu knew that his mother, Elizabeth McKenzie, had second thoughts about this move. On the second evening that they were in Glacier, she took him aside and established rules. Liz made it very clear that he was able to talk to all of the women and kids in town, but he was to avoid the grown men at all cost. She felt that this group of men was the roughest, meanest looking group she had ever seen. So it's not surprising that the first rule about not talking to the men was established. Liz added that he could be in their small cabin, or in the back part of Graham's, but not in the bar. If the benches were open out front it was okay to sit there, but if any of the "Boys" came and sat down he was to get up and leave. His mother, at this point, was questioning her decision to move to this godforsaken place. She added that they would continue to give it a try, but within a short few months they may move back to Seattle.

In front of Graham's Store, facing the Mt. Baker Highway, was a sheltered boardwalk with four weathered, wooden benches that faced the street. This location provided a grand location for viewing the different activities: tourists with teenage daughters coming and going, locals checking their daily mail, loggers stopping to fill their thermoses on the way up the mountains or stopping on the way down for their first shot to either warm up or cool down, and the Boys going from one watering hole to the other. This became one of Stu's favorite places to hang out when he wasn't working in the store or at school. Almost each afternoon some of the kids his age would show up and the stories would start to fly. When the benches were occupied by the Boys, the kids would stay away.

***

PEG LEG MAYHEAU

After being in Glacier for a few days, Stu decided it was time to try out one of the benches out front. He sat out there in the late afternoon doing the dreaded homework that none of the other kids in Glacier seemed to do. It was a beautiful fall day in Glacier, and all the mountains were out in full glory. In Seattle, clear beautiful days in the fall did occur, but it always remained foggy until after lunch. He quickly determined that there must not be fog in Glacier because those days were always clear.

All of a sudden Stu heard "thunk, thunk, thunk" footsteps approaching from down the boardwalk. He saw a man approaching him with what looked to be one normal leg and the other a wooden leg. The man approached Stu and joined him on the bench. He carried a round piece of wood and a very wicked looking hunting knife.

"Hello kid, my name is Mayheau," he said, "that's my last name, Mayheau. Everybody calls me Peg Leg and I've never been able to understand why. Oh, I see you looking at my leg. You are probably wondering what happened to me. Well, I got shot up pretty bad in the war, and they cut my leg off right there below the knee. I get around pretty well and can work most men into the ground. I have found, however, it is not very good for sneaking around."

Stu knew at this point, according to his mother's rules, he should get up and take off but this talkative man would not stop talking. Stu felt kind of trapped so he remained seated.

Peg Leg started working on the piece of wood with that big knife and continued, "I'm just making myself a new leg here. The old ones, they wear off and then I develop a very bad limp. This one here is almost finished now, and I'll attach it within a few minutes. It usually takes about 4 to 6 hours to carve a new leg."

He then added, "I always use a local wood called the vine maple. It is by far the hardest wood in this region and being so hard it takes a lot of work to get it shaped up. One thing about having a peg leg, a pair of socks lasts you a long time."

After a few minutes, he stood up having fitted the new leg just below the knee. He started walking down the boardwalk and then returned. He stated, "Well, I think I got a pretty good fit. Now I'm not limping so badly, and that's always a good sign. Think I'll give her another try." He began to walk down the boardwalk again but was not really watching where he was stepping. There was a big three-inch diameter knothole in the boardwalk that had fallen out, and as luck would have it, Mayheau put the brand-new peg leg directly in the knot hole. Tumbling forward, he hollered out, "God damnit, now look what happened! I could have broken my damn brand new leg off." He looked down to see that his brand new leg was stuck in the hole.

Peg Leg turned to Stu and said, "Hey, could you hightail it into the bar and have the Boys come out and give me a hand? Hurry up; I can't stand like this too much longer." Well, at this point Stu realized he hadn't broken any of his mother's rules as he had not spoken to the man, but what was he to do now? He had been asked to go into the bar and talk to the Boys; now that was breaking two rules! Peg Leg excitedly shouted, "Well, kid, get your ass going!"

Stu reluctantly walked into the bar feeling completely out of place and not knowing who to talk to. He said, "There's a gentleman out on the boardwalk that needs assistance with his peg leg. He got it caught in a hole and he asked me to come in and get help." Stu then realized that no one had heard a word he had said so he repeated it, this time a little louder. Now, all of the Boys quit talking and he had their full attention. Upon realizing what the young man had said, they all had an extremely first class laugh. A couple of them said that they should bring Peg Leg a drink. Stu just stood there not knowing what the next step ought to be, and he realized very quickly that the bulk of them had been drinking all day.

One guy said, "Boys, let's go give him a hand." When they all had gone out to the front of the store and saw the peg leg stuck in the hole, they sat down on the benches and had a great laugh. Stu was dumbfounded. Here was this man in dire need of assistance, and no one was taking any serious action.

Finally, Frank Bottiger said, "Hell, I'm just going to go to the truck, get the chainsaw, and cut the leg off and that piece of the leg can plug the hole permanently." Stu looked at Peg Leg and saw a very distressed look on his face.

Eventually one of them came up with a better idea, got a claw hammer, pried up and removed the board next to the one that the peg leg was in. He then reached down inside and started tapping the bottom of the new leg to drive it back up. Peg Leg started to scream at him, "God damnit, don't hit it so hard. You're going to break it and you are jarring my brains." Soon the peg leg was free and he was thanking all of the boys for their help. Peg Leg joined them in the bar for a toast to the new leg, and they left the plank removed. Stu stood outside with a look of wonderment.

JUMBO BILL

During the second month of living in Glacier, Stu was sitting on the end bench, hanging out, when around the corner from where he lived appeared Jumbo Bill. Jumbo came right up to him and sat down. In the time Stu had been in town, he had never uttered a word to Jumbo, thinking that Jumbo probably didn't know his name or that he even existed. Jumbo Bill started out, "Well, how do you like Glacier compared to Seattle? Big change. I've been to Seattle on two occasions; didn't care much for it."

Jumbo then looked to Stu for a reply. "Mr. Wilson, when my mother and I arrived here I didn't know what to think. Now that I have been here a while, I am starting to get hooked on it."

Jumbo thought for a minute then said, "Man, this here kid has more manners than the total of all the other kids in Glacier Township combined."

Jumbo Bill was from no place and lived up above the railroad tracks in a shabby little cabin with a bunch of dogs—maybe five or six. Someone in Glacier must have complained to the county sheriff about these dogs barking and running wild while Jumbo was off working. One day, a deputy sheriff arrived in town, found Jumbo's house and shot the whole pack. Jumbo was awfully upset by this action but within a couple of weeks he had a pair of dogs and set out to launch a new pack. The people of Glacier made it very clear to the deputy sheriff that he was not to be seen again in Glacier.

Jumbo Bill had no indoor plumbing in his cabin and in the summer he would utilize his outhouse, which was not a problem, but in the winter with between three and four feet of snow on the ground for months he could not get to the outhouse. Since he was becoming an elderly man, his winter time routine was used. With only a front door, Jumbo Bill would go out on the porch to relieve himself. To do the big one he would use his snow shovel, poop in the shovel, and then throw it off the front porch as far as he could. Now as winter wore on, with the snow lingering, Jumbo's yard became less and less appealing. When a neighbor would come to visit, they would stand out in the street and shout, "Jumbo, I'm

GATEWAY GROCERY–GEORGE HINTON PROPRIETOR
The Gateway Grocery was the forerunner of Graham's store. It is believed
that George Hinton constructed the building around 1906 and the Graham
Family purchased it in 1932. Note that this photo is pre-automobile days.
(Postcard Photo-Whatcom Museum, Bellingham, WA)

JUMBO BILL'S HOME
Glacier had many one room cabins such as this one for the old bachelors like
Jumbo Bill. (G. Byeman)

SCHOOL PICTURE AT GLACIER SCHOOL
The original school in the area was consolidated in the town of Glacier. A one room building was used and it contained all twelve grades. Glacier District was Washington School District No. 85. The Glacier School District had three teachers, with Hazel Bottiger as the principal, at their maximum enrollment. Then with declining enrollment, the small district was absorbed into the Maple Falls District. Later, Maple Falls was absorbed by the Mt. Baker District. (J. Steiner)

coming in! Don't flush the toilet!"

Like almost all the grown men and teen boys of Glacier, Jumbo Bill had an unbelievable love for chewing tobacco. He had a different feature than most; he had a vertical slit in his lower lip that extended from the top of the lower lip down to his chin, which was an old cut that had not healed back across. Jumbo could actually whistle through the slit, but his biggest claim to fame was that as he chewed, the tobacco would run through the slit and drip down his chin, and finally down his shirt depending on how many jumbos he drank.

Jumbo Bill was a very talented musician. It was obvious that he was self-taught and his favorite instrument was the harmonica. He would sit out on the benches in front of Graham's and when no one was around he would play

the harmonica for hours. These musical serenades would attract many of the local people and many of the children. If one particular child had a great interest in the harmonica, Jumbo would volunteer to give him lessons. Now these lessons went fine until the student took one look at the mouthpiece and saw that over half of the harmonica's cells were full of Copenhagen. At that point, each potential student returned the harmonica with a big "Thank you, but not today."

Jumbo drank nothing but jumbos of beer; not any wine or whiskey. When he was not working as a logger for Pamp Bottiger, he would sit in one of the two watering holes and drink all day. One afternoon he was sitting in Graham's drinking, when he and Earl Graham got into a debate in which

FRANK BOTTIGER'S GRAZING AREA–EXCELSIOR MEADOWS
The grazing permit issued by the Forest Service identified the area of Church Mountain and Rocky Ridge. The cattle could actually graze to the summit of Church Mountain and over into Yellow Aster Butte Meadows. Some of the cattle that may have thought they were mountain goats could also venture as far as Twin Lakes. (G. Byeman)

Jumbo said he could drink a whole case of jumbos (12) in one sitting. The debate turned into a bet, and Jumbo Bill told Earl that he would be back later to take up the bet. Jumbo went across the street to the Mt. Baker Inn, sat down and proceeded to drink 12 jumbos. After proving to himself that he could do it, he walked back across the street to Graham's and told Earl that he was ready to take on the bet.

Not having a wife or kids, Jumbo was a friend to all the children in Glacier, and they were given treats of candy which he carried for that purpose. As he became an old man he could not see to cut his finger nails and they became so long that they curved down which amused all of the kids.

Jumbo had a procedure that he always did when meeting someone for the first time in the bars. He would jump off his stool, stand very rigid, bang his heels together, then make a perfect salute to the person, and finally shake hands.

BOTTIGER CATTLE DRIVE
Today was the day. Stu had been in Glacier for a couple of months and had gotten a pretty good feel of the area and the people. He met and became good friends with three or four of the local boys most of whom were in the seventh grade. They were good guys except they were all kind of crude. Stu's mother was

30

not impressed with their profanity and was horrified to find out that a couple of them had started to use Copenhagen.

Frank Bottiger has decided that the snow in the Excelsior Meadows had melted out and that it was time for the annual Bottiger cattle drive. Each year he had to wait for the snow to melt out before taking them up into the high mountain meadows, which provided his summer pasture.

Little Pamp, the grandson of Frank Bottiger, was in downtown Glacier attempting to recruit a crew of between five and six cowhands for the drive. Little Pamp saw Little Joe and Stu so he walked toward them. "How about helping Frank, Uncle Leck, and me drive cows this afternoon?" he asked.

Stu looked at him with a questionable eye and Little Joe asked, "What's the pay this year? That four dollars last year was not enough."

Little Pamp added, "Frank said that last year after all the bitching, he decided this year the pay is five dollars." The two agreed to sign on and were told to be down at the ranch, west of town, at 1:00 PM sharp.

Before starting down to the ranch, Little Joe filled Stu in with the information about the cattle drive. Frank Bottiger had a permit from the forest service to summer 35 head of cattle up in the Excelsior Meadows each year. He drove them from the ranch up the highway to the Excelsior Trail Head and then up into the Meadows.

Little Joe gave Stu more information about the trip. They would both meet up with the other cowboys down at the corral at the ranch and would all be

FRANK BOTTIGER'S ONE-OF-A-KIND TEXAS LONGHORN COW
Frank had many different nationalities of cattle but he only had one Texas Longhorn. (F. Bottiger)

riding horses. He told Stu to ride Old Buckshot, and he would be riding the mean one called the Bastard. Stu was excited because he had never been on a horse in his life, but Little Joe told him that Buckshot was old and walked with a limp. As they were about ready to head out, Earl Graham met them at the door and said, "Stu, I got this old cowboy hat and I want you to wear it today. Too bad you don't have a bandana to cover your face." Stu looked at Little Joe who had kind of a funny smirk smile on his face, but that didn't have any meaning to him.

The boys headed down the highway with the others, the Brown brothers, Don and Bumpy Head, to get to the cattle pens at 1:00 o'clock. "Hey," Stu asked Little Joe, "where's the horses?"

Little Joe answered, "Oh, the Bottigers are bringing them."

About 2:00 o'clock, a beat-up G.M.C. pickup truck rumbled up the road with Frank, Uncle Leck, and Little Pamp in the front seat. One look at the three and Stu quickly noticed that Frank had spent the morning drinking wine, because as he got out of the truck, two empty Muscatel wine bottles hit the ground. Frank bent down, picked each up and threw them into the brush where hundreds of bottles already were. "Well, you are the saddest looking group of cowhands I have ever hired. Look, we are so hard up, we even have the City Slicker Kid," said Frank looking directly at Stu. "What in the hell is the hat for and have you ever seen the ass of a cow?" Frank excitedly then added, "Is that Clark Gable's hat from the big movie? Yes it is, that's the hat he wore when he arrived in town. Well kid, with you wearing that hat, you must think

you're going to be the next big movie star here in Glacier."

Looking at Stu, Frank continued, "I'm telling you, City Slicker Kid, you keep away from the front of that big Texas Longhorn, or he will place one of his horns right up your ass." Stu realized that the whole group was having a good laugh; then he realized they were laughing at him. Frank added, "Now as we are going through town, keep the damn cows on the road, out of people's yards and mainly their gardens."

Bumpy Head Brown stepped forward and said, "Last year we had problems with them logging trucks coming up or down the road."

Frank responded, "Get the damn trucks to stop or get the goddamn cows off the road." Stu thought that with the 200 to 300 logging trucks a day and all the other traffic, it would be interesting.

Bumpy Head said, "Ma said, 'Keep those goddamn shitters out of her garden.' "

Not seeing the horses, Stu asked Little Joe, "Where are the horses that you spoke of?" The whole group turned, looked at him and had another great laugh.

Finally Frank quit laughing and said, "Now I understand this is why you got the cowboy hat! He thinks this is Montana or something." Stu took the hat off and left it on the seat of Frank's pickup. He realized then the mode of transportation was on one's own two legs, either walking or running.

Stu realized right away that there were not 35 head of cattle; more like 50. The drive started up the road with Stu positioned on the left side. The cattle had a month or better with almost nothing to eat and they constantly wanted to stop and eat. Frank yelled out the window of the truck to keep them moving. At this rate of progress, Stu thought it would be dark before they got to the trail head. As the cattle approached the town, they could smell the fresh green grass and started to trot. The big longhorn headed directly toward the Hanson home lawn on the left with their beautiful garden. Mrs. Hanson took pride in growing the top garden in Glacier. Seeing this situation develop, Stu became concerned about keeping the cattle out; however, in his mind he kept hearing Frank's warning about "up your ass."

"God damn it, holy shit, City Slicker Kid, get that big bastard out of there," shouted Frank at the top of his lungs. Then about this time a big Kenworth logging truck with a full load approached the herd, it's brakes screaming with the smell of burnt rubber.

Stu turned toward Frank and said, "Well," and took after the longhorn at a full run. The big black bull headed into the Brown family garden and worked it over. Mrs. Brown came out of her house, and broke a half rotten 2 x 4 over the bull's back. This did nothing to stop him from eating a beautiful head of cabbage. The Brown brothers felt lucky that they were on the opposite side of the road.

Half an hour later, the hands got the cattle through Glacier with heavy deposits of cow manure throughout the town, on the main road, side streets, some of the boardwalks, and people's sidewalks. After crossing the two bridges out of town, the next stop for the cattle was the well-kept lawn in front of the ranger station. Frank said it was okay to let them graze there because he did not have any respect for the United States Forest Service; them being a form of government.

The head ranger came out on the front porch with arms crossed. He yelled out to Frank who was sitting in the truck watching the cattle eat their fill. "Frank, how about coming over here so I can speak to you?" Frank joined him on the front porch and the ranger asked, "What in the hell do you think you are doing?"

"Well," started Frank, "I have a grazing permit from the United States Forest Service which I have had since 1922. I assume that the grazing can start the moment I get into the national forest."

The new Ranger's face started to turn red and he screamed, "Frank, if you don't get those damn cows out of Glacier immediately, I will do everything in my power next year to get your grazing permit nullified. Do you understand?"

Without a word Frank walked slowly back to the pickup and hollered to the cowboys, "Move 'em out, boys."

About every five minutes, another truck would enter the scene, and the hands had to either split or drive the cows to one side to let the trucks pass. The leader of the pack was not the big black bull with the four foot long horns but a 12-year-old black and white cow named, Old Cow. Frank's cattle were not purebred animals by any means; more like every type and with a bad case of inbreeding.

Old Cow knew exactly where the trail met the highway and turned up the trail paying no attention to the Forest

UNITED STATES DEPARTMENT OF AGRICULTURE
FOREST SERVICE

GRAZING PERMIT
(This permit is not transferable)

July 11, 1922
(Date.)

M r. F. E. Bottiger _____, of _____ Glacier, Wash _____, having paid
(Name)   (Place of residence.)

to the Portland/ Branch, Federal Reserve
National Bank of San Francisco, Portland, Ore
(U. S. Depository)

the grazing fee amounting to the sum of _____ seven and 50/100 _____ dollars

($ 7.50 _____), is hereby authorized to pasture the following number and class of live stock:

_____ 15 _____ head of _____ cattle

and _____ head of _____

branded or earmarked as follows:

(Right.)   (Left.)

upon lands of the United States within the _____ Washington _____ National Forest

from _____ July 15, _____, 1922, to _____ Sept. 15, _____, 1922;

Provided, That the animals shall not intrude upon any area upon which grazing is prohibited, nor upon any portion of the National Forest except the following-described area:

_____ Church Mt. and Rocky Ridge _____

This permit is issued upon the facts stated and under the promises and agreements made by said

_____ F. E. Bottiger _____ in his application dated _____ June 25th _____, 1922,
and subject to the stipulations printed on the back hereof.

This permit is issued with no obligation or agreement on the part of the Government to maintain an exclusive possession upon any part of said Forest to any one person or firm, nor as to adjustment of any conflict as to possession.

For a violation of any of the terms of the application on which it is based, or whenever any injury is being done the Forest by reason of the presence of the animals therein, this permit will be revoked and the animals will be removed from the Forest.

_____
Supervisor.

NOTE.—Animals under six months old at the time of entry, which are the natural increase of stock grazed under permit, will not be counted.

F.E. BOTTIGER GRAZING PERMIT
Frank Bottiger first received the permit in 1922 and held the right until 1955.
(National Archives and Records Administration-Seattle, WA)

FRANK BOTTIGER CATTLE IN EXCELSIOR MEADOWS
This grazing permit allowed Bottiger to graze his cattle from Church Mountain to Yellow Aster Butte Meadows. This was a distance of between eight and nine miles. (F. Bottiger)

Service trail sign. All 49 of the cattle followed the old girl, and she then led them all the way to the top of the ridge, high above the Nooksack River. With this turn, the annual drive was over, and all the hands piled into the back of the pickup and down to town with Uncle Leck driving.

Getting back to town, Uncle Leck paid each cowboy his wage. Each of them was tired. They thought that next year they would demand six dollars. When Stu headed home, he looked back and old Frank was still in the pickup, sound asleep. He realized that his sneakers were not to be used again.

Stu gathered up Clark's hat and slowly walked into Graham's to replace it on the top shelf. Old Earl came into the room with a big smile on his face and asked, "How was the cattle drive and how was your horse?" Stu knew that old Earl was part of the joke, so

he added very quickly that it was great and the horse was the best. He walked over to see his mother who immediately asked Stuart how was the cattle drive.

He answered, "All had a great time. Everybody had a great big laugh." Slowly the City Slicker Kid headed home to the cabin out the back door of Graham's.

The next week, Little Pamp came to find Stu and ask if he was interested in making a few bucks the next day. Pamp told him that he and Bill Brown were hiking up to Excelsior Meadows at 2:00 in the afternoon. An airplane that Frank hired in Bellingham was going to drop four 50 lb. blocks of salt for the cows by parachutes. Pamp said that they needed a third guy and wanted to know if Stu wanted to come.

The three of them got a ride from Frank to the trailhead, then started hiking up the trail. Little Pamp and Bill

**UPON THEIR ARRIVAL, THE CATTLE ARE ALREADY
SEARCHING FOR FOOD**
The people of Glacier always said that Bottiger Cattle had shorter legs in the
front quarters. (F. Bottiger)

WINCHESTER FIRE LOOKOUT
The Excelsior Lookout looked very much like the Winchester Lookout in this
old photo with the same amount of wear and tear. (J. Hanson)

Brown started out hiking like they had a bear chasing them. All of a sudden Stu remembered that he was going to have a conversation with his mother about buying some heavy-duty shoes, but here he was going up the hillside with sneakers again.

Stu realized that when he stood on the boardwalk in front of Graham's, these Excelsior Meadows do not look so far away, but after hiking for two hours he was exhausted. As they reached the tree line, Stu could not believe the beauty of the mountains, with Baker and Shuksan to the south and the border peaks to the north.

The three were up at the proposed drop site by 12:30 and ate a mother-created wonderful lunch which Stu shared with the black flies and mosquitoes. The plane was on time, made a pass, and came back for the drop. The plane went directly over their heads and out came the load; a beautiful site. The only problem was that the wind was blowing from the south and the loads drifted 1000 feet down the north side of the ridge.

Pamp said, "God damn pilot isn't worth a shit, and now we have to find the salt blocks and carry them up to Excelsior Fire Lookout." The Bottiger grazing lease with the Forest Service may or may not have given them the use of the fire lookout to store things like salt for the cattle. Each block weighed 50 lbs. They located and carried the blocks which took the rest of the afternoon. The three hurried down the trail to be picked up at the trail head. When they arrived, of course, there was no Frank as he had stayed at one of the watering holes to drink and forgot about them. The three hitched a ride with a logging truck back to town.

As Stu limped into Graham's to see his mother, she took one look at him and said, "Stuart, did you slip and fall? Are you hurt badly?"

"No mother," Stuart replied, "but mom, I must get some mountain shoes and burn these sneakers."

In the early years Frank, or one of his two sons, would hike up and check the cows two or three times a summer. In later years, the cows were forgotten until fall. The black and white cow, Old Cow, would determine when it was right to return and she would lead them back to the ranch. Their return could be in the middle of the day or in the middle of night. If it was night, she would lead them directly through town (stopping at Hanson's and Brown's gardens for a few fall treats) and into the corral at the ranch. Sometimes they returned when there was fresh snow on the ridge or when they ran out of grass.

One of the Brown brothers told Stu that one year Frank sold off the black and white cow. When fall came, without that cow, the cattle went down the north side to Damfino Lakes. When they did not return, Frank went searching and found them in the head waters of Canyon Creek. With the high ridges snowed shut, he, with a crew of two others, had to clear out the Canyon Creek Trail so they could get the cattle home.

FISHING TRIP

A few months later, Stu was doing the Saturday afternoon work in the back room of Graham's as directed by his mother, the head cook. A little past 3:00 PM, the door bolted open and slammed against the back wall. Stu's friend, Little Joe, stood in the door way and said excitedly, "Remember, I told you the Boys go fishing about this time each year? Well I heard them yapping about it over at the Inn." The Mt. Baker Inn was another eating and watering hole located across the street from Graham's. The Boys alternated drinking in one of the two. When a man's tab got too high at one, he would move to the other.

"I will go clear it with my mother, and I'll meet you out front in 15 minutes," said Stu as his excitement grew.

Little Joe was ten minutes late and he bitched about his mother. "The old lady wanted me to do this or that and all these things that could wait until tomorrow. Then I promised to bring home some fresh fish, and she changed her mood. Damn well better bring home some fish."

After thinking a little, Stu added, "You know, I have never been fishing in my life—don't know a thing about it. Where we lived in Seattle there was no place to fish. Oh, lots of water but no place near our house. I don't even have a fishing pole or any gear." He threw his arms in the air and looked at Little Joe.

Little Joe replied, "When we see the Boys leave the Inn and go down to Pamp's shop for their gear, we will head up to Thompson Creek on our bikes."

As they were waiting, Stu asked again about the gear and Little Joe told him that he would see. After about half an hour, out came five guys from the side door of the Inn, each with either a bottle of wine or a six pack of beer. They piled into an old logging pickup and headed

off to get their gear. The 12-year-old boys took off as fast as they could to beat the Boys to the fishing hole.

Arriving at the site before the Boys, Stu and little Joe hid in the brush near the creek and waited their arrival. Thompson Creek was the high point up the Nooksack River where Sockeye Salmon returned to spawn; a relatively small creek with deep pools, which are ideal for the cycle of these Pacific salmon. Little Joe had told Stu that once the fishermen arrived and got busy, being half drunk they would not notice them being there.

Upon the Boys arrival, as they started to unload the gear, Leck Bottiger and Jumbo Bill appeared to be the most experienced fisherman. Leck commented that there were no fresh tire tracks in the muddy road and that they would have the creek to themselves. Stu asked Little Joe, "What kind of fishing tackle is this that comes in wood boxes and rolls of wire? It's not anything I have seen before."

Little Joe answered, "I thought that you hadn't fished?"

"I played with my grandfather's pole in the back yard," replied Stu.

The young kids watched as the five men prepared the gear, drank beer, and spit chew constantly. Stu saw something being thrown into the water. After a few seconds a loud sound was made, K-BOOM!

The first fishing lure went off, with water, limbs, small trees, and fish flying all over. This K-BOOM was repeated up and down the creek bed with the same effect. By this time, the Boys were cheering and slapping each other on their backs.

"It's time to join the Boys," said

Little Joe as they walked out of the bushes like they were part of their party.

In seeing them, Leck directed, "Get yourself a gunny sack out of the truck and go find the sockeyes."

Loading up the truck for the return trip down to Glacier, one of the Boys told the kids to throw their bikes in the back. After parking in front of Graham's, Leck ordered, "Ok, lets take these six sacks of fish into the watering hole here and divide them so everyone around gets fresh fish. You two kids come on in too and I will buy a soda for your help." That night almost every family in Glacier had fresh fish and within a couple of hours the smell of smoked fish was filling the air of Glacier.

Upon arriving back at Graham's, Little Joe was so excited to share their experiences with Stu's mother. He excitedly said, "Damn, we did good fishing, and you will love these fish Stu and I have already cleaned. Oh, sorry about the swearing—the damn."

She replied to Stu, "Was it hard to catch the fish, son?"

Stu looked over and gave Little Joe a wink, and said, "I couldn't catch a single one and they were using DuPont Spinners."

Outside on the board walk, Stu asked Little Joe, "Was that method of fishing today up at the creek lawful?"

Little Joe answered, "There is no law east of the Warnick Bridge."

JERRY'S ROCK

Little Joe and Stu were walking the main street of Glacier on a dull, late Saturday afternoon. As they neared Graham's corner, a beat up car stopped

and out piled Jerry Bourn looking like he had a full load of drink. Jerry struggled to get up on the boardwalk, using the wall to find the door to Graham's as he entered. Little Joe started up a conversation, "Well, I don't think Jerry will be inside long today. They will throw his sorry ass out." Within five minutes, Jerry was led out the door, told to go home, and sober up. Jerry went over to the end bench, lay down and took a nap.

Little Joe looked over at him and said, "Jerry won't sleep long; he will get up and go back inside."

Sure enough in a few minutes, he was up and went back inside. This time as he was quickly escorted out, he took a hard fall on the boardwalk. He got up fighting mad, headed around the corner and up toward the train station. In a few minutes, he returned carrying a rock so large that a normal man could not have picked it up. Along the side of the depot was a pile of such sized rocks and Jerry must have remembered their location. He labored with the rock, to get it up on the boardwalk, and got near the windows of the bar. He took a couple of steps back and lunged foward. His intent was to throw the large rock through the window, however, he forgot to let go. He went through the glass window right along with the rock.

Little Joe said, "That was exciting!"

Jerry came out 15 minutes later with a large towel, soaked with blood wrapped around his head. Now he did seem more sober and he headed up the highway toward home.

COUNTRY CREDIT

One day Stu asked, "Earl, tell me about this credit thing that you give the local people."

"Well, it's kind of the way that you do business out in the rural area. If you go along with the people and extend them credit, they will usually be a very faithful customer. Now in the wintertime when the loggers are on rocking chair, they have very little income coming in, but when they go back to work in the spring, they will always pay back their winter-created debt. You're probably wondering what I mean by rocking chair?"

"Rocking chair is unemployment income that the loggers get when they cannot work. Now, I have a little story to tell you about two of our local boys that were given credit down at the Kendall Store.

"Leck and Glen Rannkin were logging one spring over on Slide Mountain. From Glacier, to get to Slide Mountain each day, they had to drive down the Mt. Baker Highway to Welcome and cross the river. Every morning they would stop at the Kendall Store and charge a half-case of beer and a six-pack of wine. On the return trip, they did the same, half a case of beer and a six-pack of wine.

"After one month, Leck stated that he was going to stop and pay his grocery bill. When he returned to the truck, Glen asked, 'How much was the bill?'

"Leck said, 'Not bad, $35.45. Oh, and by the way, I did buy one loaf of bread last month.' "

Year Number Two

GLACIER INN IN GLACIER, WASHINGTON
Glacier Inn later became the Gateway Inn followed by the Graham's Store.
Note: We now have autos and gas pumps. (E. Morgenthaler)

EARL'S MARKETING PLAN

About this time, Earl Graham came out of the store and stood on the corner of the boardwalk looking up at the meadows on Church Mountain through field glasses. Now, this being a crystal clear day, all the mountain tops and ridges were out in full glory. Stu could not see what Earl was looking at and finally whispered to Jumbo, "What is he looking at?"

Jumbo answered, "Hold on, you will see."

Soon a car load of tourists came through slowly heading to Baker, and seeing Earl they pulled over in front of the store and got out. Soon, they were gathered about Earl taking turns looking through the field glasses. Earl directed them, "Look right on the ridge or down that gulch. Oh maybe they are out of sight now." Earl explained that he had been watching mountain goats all morning, and soon two additional cars stopped with everybody out looking up at Church Mountain. Earl is telling them that in about an hour the goats should be back in full view. Oh, by the way inside here, we serve the best burgers in town." Earl suggested they all move inside.

Jumbo then said, "Great trick, that

41

MT. BAKER INN IN DOWNTOWN GLACIER
Mt. Baker Inn was located across the street from Graham's and the two were major competitors. Mt. Baker Inn burned down two or three times. As one can see, the Inn served as one of Glaciers last hotels. (Michael Sullivan Papers-CPNS Western Washington University, Bellingham, WA)

old Earl has to get them to stop; great marketing, and there has never been goats seen on this side of Church Mountain in years.

"Now Kid, old Earl there is not one to want any competition within twenty miles of his establishment. Why, no matter who the owner or operator is across the street, old Earl is not very friendly. Occasionally, you can catch them arguing in the middle of the street. A few years ago, he painted red dots down the middle of the road between them, and yelled, 'You stay over there you son of a bitch!' " With this Jumbo got up and headed for the door to have a beer.

BROWN FAMILY PUNISHMENT

Stu was reading at his favorite spot, the bench, and suddenly his friend Little Joe appeared. Little Joe said that there

was some kind of a commotion taking place down in the Brown's yard. He was heading down and wondered if Stu wanted to go. Stu's immediate answer was, "Of course, I'll come right now."

When they got down in front of the Brown's house, they found a group of small children gathered along the fence in the front yard. As they approached, they saw the victim that was causing all the laughter. Stu quizzed Joe, "What in the world is going on and why is that little boy dressed like that?"

Little Joe answered, "Well, this Brown kid, who is about five years old, is being punished by one of Mrs. Brown's standard methods. This little guy must've been misbehaving. She has found that if she dresses the boys up in a dress with girl's shoes for the day and ties them to a post in the front yard that usually takes care of the problem. With all the neighborhood kids coming

MT. BAKER INN BURNING IN 1950
Earl Graham would have had an inner smile when he was watching the fire destroy his competitor. (Jack Carver-Whatcom Museum, Bellingham, WA)

by standing on the street and laughing their heads off, whatever the bad deed was it will never be done again. Well, don't ask me about the daughter's punishment because I don't know."

LARS RYE

"Well, Mr. Wilson, tell me about Lars Rye," asked Stu one morning sitting on the bench with his old friend.

First taking a fresh plug of tobacco, Jumbo slowly started the story, "Lars came from nowhere; maybe the old country, yes, I think so. After he arrived in town, he settled down on the river north of town, beside Pamp Bottiger's land. Did he own the land and just live there? No one knew. He lived down

there in a one room cabin. He had a couple of cows, pigs, and some chickens with a small lean-to of a barn connected to an old fir stump. Each day, he would walk up town to sell milk or eggs— sometimes firewood and get his mail. While in town, he would buy two ice cream cones—one for himself and one for his dog. When they were both done, they would head home.

"Lars lived down in a small one room cabin on the banks of the Nooksack River. When he started to live down there and when he left, no one knows. The stove in his cabin didn't have a stovepipe connected to the chimney, the pipe had been burnt through and was discarded, and soon he was living in what was like a smoke house. This condition worsened and when you

43

LARS RYE AT HOME WITH HIS DOG
(F. Bottiger)

would see him his skin was the color of smoke-like smoked meat. His one set of wool clothes matched his hide. Under his pants and shirt, he wore the same long, wool, one-piece underwear suit year-round. This smoky living condition went on for years. One time I went down to visit, and I could not believe that any person could live in these conditions. When I was there he had finished eating, so he set his plate on the floor, and his old dog licked it clean. He then put it up in the cupboard—all clean. Oh, by the way everybody in town called the dog, Smokey.

"A few years later, he became very ill and Pamp Bottiger, who had been taking care of him, decided that he should be taken to the county hospital out there north of Bellingham. Upon checking him in, Pamp was informed of his grave condition. Thinking that the old man was to die, he decided to go to Bellingham and buy him some new clothes. Pamp, being concerned and upset by the old man's condition,

decided he better stop by his favorite Bellingham watering hole, the Horseshoe, and have a few.

"Following the purchasing of the clothes, he returned to the county hospital. He was taken aside by the head nurse, was told that some of the medication seemed to be working; however, he would be there for a long period of time. Pamp left the new clothes assuming that if Lars did die, he could be buried in them."

"As Pamp was leaving the hospital, the head nurse approached him again. She informed him that Lars had been wearing the long underwear for so long that his body hair had grown completely through it. She stated that it was hard to determine what was black wool and what was his hair. She also said that they were trying to get it cut away but it was very difficult and very painful for him. Pamp informed her that he had to get going, but please keep him informed, not expecting to hear anything.

LARS RYE'S HEAD STONE AT THE GLACIER CEMETERY
Lars was born in Norway and served in the Spanish-American War as a Pvt. 3 Wis. Infantry. (G. Byeman)

"A few months later, the boys were sitting in Graham's having their normal social hour. In came a complete stranger and he sat down at the bar. Pamp, Jumbo Bill, and the others tried to figure out the story behind who this individual was and why he was in Glacier. Finally, Jumbo Bill stood up and said, 'I'm referred to as Jumbo Bill and I would like to meet you.'

"The stranger then said, 'It's me, Jumbo, don't you recognize me?'

"Finally, with a puzzled look on Jumbo's face, Pamp stepped forward and quickly said, 'I'll be damned, it's you Lars Fry, and the only reason I recognize you is because of the clothes that I bought you!' Everybody joined in for a joyous reunion for Lars who was truly welcomed back to Glacier.

"Lars never lived in the smoke house again. He lived in a boarding house in Glacier until he died two years later.

"He told me that at one time he was employed with the Mt. Baker Club surveying and mapping up on Mt. Baker and Shuksan about 1910 or maybe 1915. He also said that he fought in the Spanish War. Oh, you know he is buried up at the grave yard. Fine old guy; didn't say a hell of a lot," Jumbo reminisced. With that Jumbo got up and headed inside for his beer.

FRANK BOTTIGER

Earl asked Stu, "What's with all your interest in Frank Bottiger? Why don't you ask him yourself?"

In the time that Stu had lived in Glacier, he had reached a point where he could talk to all the Boys, except Frank. The only time that Frank talked to him was to call him City Slicker Kid. Stu worked for Earl at Graham's Store following school each day and also during the summer break. Since

GATEWAY TO GLACIER AND FOURTH OF JULY PREPARATION
Mt. Baker Highway was a one lane road. The author questions what the line is that runs on the left side of the road. This location is near where the Glacier School was located. (CPNWS Western Washington University, Bellingham, WA)

Earl Graham's children were full-grown and had relocated away from Glacier, Stu had grown to be an especially close friend. Often the two talked about many different subjects and Stu became extremely curious about the history of Glacier. "All right, I will tell you but it may take a few hours," added Earl.

"Frank Bottiger's older sister, named Julia, was married to Leslie Haggard, who owned the Haggard Store in Maple Falls. Haggard built his first store, however, in Glacier, in about 1905. Frank became, through his sister, a partner/operator and took up residence here. That building was built about the time of this store and it was located around the corner but on this side of the Mountain Home Hotel."

He continued, "In his early twenties, Frank was a striking looking fellow, not very tall but with broad shoulders and strong leadership qualities. The Glacier School had a young unmarried teacher here by the name of Hazel. A courtship started between the two, and in a short time the two were married. Now the two were the flashiest couple in Glacier with him being part owner of a store and her being one of three school teachers. They were an extremely social couple and were involved in countless activities of the town, Glacier Township government, and school positions. The two would be off to places like Sedro Woolley where Frank's family lived. The Maple Falls Leader newspaper had numerous stories of the two traveling by

46

**MAIN INTERSECTION OF GLACIER IS READY TO
CELEBRATE THE FOURTH OF JULY**
This is the main meeting point in town with the train depot and the Mountain
Home Hotel to the left. Note the wood benches to the left of center. (T. Warger)

THE SAME INTERSECTION IN GLACIER LOOKING EAST
Note the road surface of the Mt. Baker Road and also at Graham's the road
turned to the left with a building directly ahead in the path of the present
highway. (G. Byeman)

LESLIE AND FRANK BOTTIGER–SISTER AND BROTHER
Photo was taken at Kinsey Studio in Sedro Woolley. Darius Kinsey was one of
the most noted photographers of the logging industry. (F. Bottiger)

FRANK AND HAZEL BOTTIGER IN THE BACK SEAT OF A CAR
The young man in front of the car was about ready to crank her over. It looks like a major job for a young man of his age, and one wonders why Frank doesn't get out and crank the car himself. (F. Bottiger)

**FRANK AND HAZEL BOTTIGER ON ONE OF
THEIR MANY TRAIN TRIPS**
The location of this photo is unknown. (F. Bottiger)

B.B. & B.C. RAILROAD BRIDGE #4
This bridge is located at the entrance of the Saar Creek Canyon in route from Sumas to Glacier. (Whatcom Museum, Bellingham, WA)

GLACIER B.B. & B.C. RAILROAD ENGINE HOUSE
(J. Steiner)

FIRST AND IMPROVED MT. BAKER HIGHWAY

Both photos were taken between Maple Falls and Glacier. The original Maple Falls and Glacier Road was constructed by township government funding. As the area progressed, Whatcom County became involved in the road construction and maintenance. As one can see, the first roadway was very primitive. The lower photo showing the highway is 1918. (J. Steiner)

HAGGARD'S ADVERTISEMENT IN MAPLE FALLS LEADER NEWSPAPER IN 1920
The Glacier store was much smaller than the Maple Falls store and lasted for a few years. The Maple Falls building burned down in 1987 when it was owned by Wayne Beech. (Maple Falls Leader)

train out of Glacier or by car as Frank was one of the first to own a car in Glacier.

"Frank was wise with his money and soon had purchased a large parcel of farm land down on Cornell Creek from old Cornell himself, which was part of his homestead claim. He improved the house, constructed additional buildings, and cleared additional land. Hazel moved down from Glacier. The couple, over the next ten years, had three children: Henry, Leslie, and Janet. You know them as Pamp, Leck, and Janet. Yes, the three that you know today."

Stu butted in and said, "Earl, I can't believe you are talking about the Bottiger family that I know so well."

Earl continued, "Now just hold your horses and listen to the whole story."

Earl stopped talking for a few moments and was in deep thought. Then he started in again, "Now old Frank's booze problems started years ago in a different manner. A few days ago in cleaning out a drawer in the office, I found an old newspaper. There were actually three different articles all within one week in November of 1912. As you may of heard, Frank was some kind of a partner in the L.E. Haggard Store here in Glacier."

The story continued, "Frank was arrested on two counts, the first being the operation of a "blind pig" and secondly for assault. The blind pig charge is the result of illegal sales of booze and the second charge, the assault charge, is the result of an issue between Frank and A. Branin, who operated a competing store. Frank was convicted of the blind pig charge and was fined $391.60. In regards to the third degree assault charge, he was acquitted and set free. So as you can see, Frank has had all kinds of problems with booze."

Stu couldn't resist and jumped in with a question, "Okay Earl, the obvious question, what in the world does a blind pig have to do with booze?"

"The term," Earl continued "blind pig was established and became a law in regards to selling of illegal alcohol. Now, the Haggard Store probably did not have any form of a license for selling alcohol. What an operator like Frank would do was stage some kind of an event in the establishment, charge to see the event, and give complimentary alcohol. Obviously, the first event must have been to see a blind pig. Frank probably did not use the blind pig scheme, but he did have hogs down at the farm. No, I never did run a blind pig program.

"Their store soon was second rate to Graham's Store, and a few years later it burned completely, along with half of the town. At the time of the fire, Frank was starting to drink heavily and he, with others, could do nothing but watch her burn. The boys decided to go drink some home brew as the fire was dying down. Well Frank, as normal, had drunk a little bit too much and started for home. He stopped at the burning remains for a last look, tripped, and took a header into the remains, falling face first. He fell on a hard object and burned a hole in his forehead. He then high tailed to get medical help from Hazel but at this time she was so upset with him she refused to help. To his dying day he had a brand in the middle of his forehead. Oh damn, for I'm ahead of myself here.

"A show of Frank's leadership occurred in about 1916 or 1917, way

CHET McKENZIE'S PACK TRAIN LEAVING GLACIER FOR GOLD FIELDS
(Whatcom Museum, Bellingham, WA)

before my time. I came to town in 1932. Now, you have heard of the Lone Jack, the abandoned gold mine up east of Shuksan. Well, back in 1916 the Boundary Gold Co. had leased and was operating the "Jack." Upon ceasing operation for the winter, the manager hired two local men to prevent any thievery from occurring over the winter, as it had in past years. Martin Orner, a likeable sort of Swede who had been employed up at the mine, and Tony Copan, an Italian fellow, were hired for this winter job.

"Now, Orner and Copan were to receive no salary, but in lieu of a salary, the two were free to mine and mill gold by hand while at the site. The two also had free access to company stores in the cookhouse. As winter approached, the two men said farewell to all their friends in Glacier and headed out to establish housekeeping for six months of winter at the Jack.

"Now, these two foreign men with contrasting blood, features, and language were to pass the long winter by themselves, with only the gold in the mine as keeper of the peace. You ever hear of cabin fever?"

"On a rainy day in the spring, an exhausted, bedraggled Copan arrived at the McDonald's Store—now the store you're sitting in. After the men greeted Copan, the next obvious question from all was: 'Where is Orner?' Copan answered slowly with a strong Italian accent, that Orner went out hunting for fresh meat three weeks ago and did not return. Copan stated that he had gone and searched for the next few days-no tracks or anything. Then Copan returned to town with his story, his personal gear, and the total gold that the two had recovered. The next day a deputy from the Sheriff's office in Bellingham arrived in town and talked to Copan in length. Since nothing

**FRANK BOTTIGER STANDING ON THE ROOF OF
THE HOTEL GLACIER**
**The building to the far left of Frank is the Forest Service Ranger Residence
and the other building is the Drake Store with Church Mountain in the
background. (P. Maiers)**

SOME OF THE BOYS OF GLACIER
**Frank Bottiger is second from the left–others not known. The group is
standing in the middle of Vaughn Street which ran north-south with the Boys
facing south toward the train depot. (J. Steiner)**

GLACIER DEPOT

The Glacier Depot, being the last one, was one of the most modern depots constructed on the B.B. & B.C. railroad line. The Depot was used for a number of years and then a major city fire destroyed it with half of the town. The railroad reconstructed the building to match exactly the first building. (Whatcom Museum, Bellingham, WA)

HOTEL GLACIER

The Hotel Glacier was the second hotel constructed in Glacier. This building was constructed by Charlie Bourn and was intended for a different clientele. It was intended for tourists and professional people. It had a tennis court which was unheard of, particularly in Glacier. (C. Kvistad)

EARLY HOTEL GLACIER
Both Hotel Glacier and Mountain Home Hotel were on Vaughn Street. The
Hotel Glacier was destroyed by fire in 1937. (C. Kvistad)

**PEOPLE RETURNING UP THE STREET TO THE DEPOT
FROM HOTEL GLACIER**
Note, the local people turning to give the tourists the look. (T. Warger)

**THE HOTEL GLACIER LATER BECAME
THE MOUTAIN HOME HOTEL**
Following the devastating fire to the Mountain Home Hotel, the Jacobs moved
down the street and took over Hotel Glacier. (M.Impero)

MOUNTAIN HOME HOTEL
This photo appears to be staged or some kind of an event. (W. Gannaway)

was found to doubt the word of Copen, he told the Boys there was nothing he could do but he might hike into the site the following summer.

"Now, Orner had many friends in Glacier as he made his home here. One friend was Frank Bottiger, and he with other Glacierites felt that Copan was hiding the truth. So, a group of Orner's friends, headed by Frank, decided to perform their own investigation of the "Jack incident" and intended to have Copen return with them. Copan indicated that he was cleared by the Deputy and he was not going back. Bottiger forcefully persuaded him to return with the group. Upon searching for a few days and seeing nothing that indicated any type of foul play, Frank and the Boys had to return to Glacier and release Copan to freedom. Within a couple days, Copan slipped out of Glacier with both shares of gold and was gone for good.

"A few years later, Bert Lowry, yes the Bert you know, was prospecting in the area and traveled to the now quiet Jack for a look at things. Entering the Lulu shaft with a light, he saw a floating body in a mined out hole, which was full of water. He quickly recalled old Martin's disappearance. The body had been tied with ropes to large rocks and thrown into the water hole. With the passing of time, the rope had rotted and the body floated to the surface. Old Martin looked good because of being in cold water for years.

"Bert returned to Glacier and again the Boys, led by Frank, headed up to the Jack. They removed the body and placed Orner in a shallow rocky grave on the side of Bear Mountain. Within a few years no one knew the location of old Orner's grave. They came back to town and notified the sheriff who placed a state wide search for Copan but no trace was ever found. You can see that the Frank of today is not the Frank of years ago.

"Now Frank had his hand in many business ventures ranging from real estate, land clearing, stores, and construction, however Frank had changed. You didn't see him and Hazel together, and he spent almost all of his time here in Graham's or the Inn with the Boys.

"He focused on all types of construction, acting as the general contractor and performing road work. In the construction of the Mt. Baker Highway, Frank had a contract to provide water culverts, both concrete and pipe types, under the roadbed. Part of Frank's work was the construction of concrete box culverts to handle small creeks. Frank became a first-rate drinking buddy with the project inspector, and by noon he would have the inspector quite drunk. Frank's crew was mixing the concrete at the site and when the inspector could no longer count, Frank would reduce the volume of cement being put in the concrete. The construction required concrete for the bottom, walls and the roof of the box culverts.

"Following the concrete curing time, the crew would remove the forms and shortly thereafter the traffic was directed over the structure. In one of the structures, the first truck over the structure collapsed it and the truck ended up in the creek. On this one occasion Frank had cut the cement back too far.

"For many years after the first

opening of the highway in 1921, the highway maintenance crew found that in a number of cases the water did not drain through the pipe culverts and they assumed that they were plugged. In digging up the roadway and the pipe, they found that Frank had only used the ends of the pipe with nothing connecting them.

"There is a story of Frank, Pamp, and Leck doing some logging up Glacier Creek in the middle of the winter. Now this was not normal because Frank did not work as a logger, but on this particular day they were working together. Frank was down by the edge of the creek bucking a log, when he slipped and fell into the water and was washed down stream. He got himself out but he was on the opposite side from his sons. With a foot of snow on the ground and being completely soaking wet, Frank yelled for help. The boys stopped working and went down on the opposite side, but could not stop laughing. They yelled across, 'It's quitting time; we're going to Graham's to warm up,' so they left Frank wet and cold, got in the pickup, and left.

"About two hours later, with complete darkness, Frank walked into Graham's and started beating on each of his sons. All the other Boys stood back and watched them roll around on the floor, knocking over chairs and tables. After a few minutes of fighting, the three of them sat at the bar drinking and laughing about it.

"In the early days, old Frank had an old work horse which was called Snot Nose. Now the old horse was big and could pull a hell of a turn of logs. Well, old Snot Nose got his name because his nose was always dripping snot. If someone new didn't know the old horse and went to pet him, Snot Nose would wipe his nose dripping down the front of their clothes. Really pissed off some new people with new clothes.

"Within a short time, Frank became what you see now today. Hazel booted him off the farm, and she became the sole owner. He moved up to town and lived with Leck. Hazel's farmhouse burned down so she moved into a separate house here in Glacier.

"Well, I guess we better get back to work and quit all this BS. I suggest that you go ahead and begin a conversation with Frank, if he is sober, and you will find him to be a very interesting and intelligent man. God, what Frank might've been if the booze hadn't got a hold of him," Earl said finishing the conversation and returning to work.

***

CALL OF THE WILD

Stu was sitting on his favorite bench in front of Graham's reading Earl's copy of "The Call of the Wild." Stu was really into the book with its connection to Glacier. He had seen pictures of Clark Gable and Loretta Young which were displayed in Graham's. Earl had told him the two had shacked up in the two story house across from the store. As a young teenage boy, Stu was intrigued and excited with that story.

Stu detected that someone was looking over his shoulder and turned to find Frank Bottiger looking down at him. Frank said, "I want to thank you for helping me up last night after falling off the deck here into the Mt. Baker Highway. You may have thought it was the booze that made me fall, but it's this

Photo by J. W. Sandison
Whatcom Museum #4842

**CLARK GABLE, LORETTA YOUNG, AND JACK OAKIE
ALL STARS IN THE MOVIE "THE CALL OF THE WILD"**
This photo is taken up in Heather Meadows, which was one of three local sites.
One of the other sites was down at Jerry Bourn's cabin at Shuksan and the
other down on the Nooksack River near the mouth of Boulder Creek.
(Wilbur Sandison-Whatcom Museum, Bellingham, WA)

HERD OF SHEEP AS ACTORS IN THE MOVIE "WOLF FANG"
The herd of sheep were unloaded from Sedro Woolley and then driven up
Highway #9 and the Mt. Baker Highway to Heather Meadows. (J. Steiner)

61

**MOUNTAIN CABIN AND WOMEN FROM ONE OF
THE THREE MOVIES**

Many temporary buildings and structures were constructed for each movie
set. (J. Steiner)

**THE CONSTRUCTED TOWN SITE IN THE MOVIE
"THE BARRIER" AT HEATHER MEADOWS**

The Heather Inn was remodeled on the outside in the making of "The
Barrier." All of the structures other than the one in the far back were
temporary structures built for the movie and were removed upon the finishing
of filming. (W. Ganaway)

piss-poor lighting here in town. Say, after I fell last night did you steal my watch?"

Stu answered, "No, Mr. Bottiger, I did not take your watch."

Frank responded, "Oh hell, I could have left the damn thing any place. So you're reading 'The Call of The Wild.' Hell, I knew them all. Clark and me were the best of drinking buddies. He is the only fellow that could match me —drink for drink, and that broad was a fine looking woman and the best to ever be in Glacier. All of the guys followed her around like little dogs.

"Clark worked his best to get me a major part in the 'Call' but there were all kinds of problems with the unions and all. I had a part in the movie. You saw the show and that fellow getting bit by that big black dog, that was me. They all said I did great and with a little luck I should be in Hollywood now instead of sitting in this hell hole of a place.

"The whole making of the thing only took three weeks to a month to shoot. Some of the film was shot down at Boulder Creek, and also up at Jerry Bourn's cabin on the river, but most of it was shot at the Meadows. They made a small town and had hundreds of people working up there. The Glacier people were positive that they were going to make Glacier 'Hollywood North' but in a week or so all of it was all gone. By the way, there were two other movies made here-one being 'The Barrier' and the other 'Wolf Fang'. All three were black and white movies and 'Wolf Fang' being the first, was also a silent movie. They were here in 1934 making the 'Call of the Wild.'

"Oh, one other thing about the movie, the last night the producer was in town, the two of us were over at the Inn having a few farewell drinks. He told me that Graham's had provided all of the food and the housing for all of the people involved. He then said that he would never do that again, because he had figured that the Graham's had severely gouged him."

As Frank got up and went into the bar, Stu said to himself, "I can't believe that Earl and Mrs. Earl would not have been fair. Frank is not a bad fellow, all you do is talk to him first thing in the morning and I mean before 9:00."

TONY IN GRAHAM'S

In his second year in Glacier, Stu worked all types of jobs for Earl. With a big crowd in Graham's, Stu acted as a guard and kept an eye on the doors, windows, and gas pumps. His main position was at the gas pumps, which was on the boardwalk out front. He did all the gas pumping and oil checking.

One Saturday in late summer, the town was hopping with people going to and from Heather Meadows, hiking all the trails, and early bear hunting season had opened. Jerry Bourn was in town. Earl was pleased to see that he had chosen the Inn for his serious drinking. Jerry had been up in the mountains for two to three weeks. He had gone prospecting up the Keep Cool Trail, crossed Excelsior Ridge, down to Damfino Lakes, and out the Canyon Creek Trail. With Jerry was his full troop of five dogs, and his horse, One Eye Tony. All were patiently standing outside the Inn waiting for Jerry's return.

**CHARLIE BOURN'S BOB
AND PINTO
(C. Kvistad)**

Being concerned about Jerry, Earl said to Stu, "Keep me informed about Jerry's whereabouts this afternoon. I expect that he will get booted out of the Inn, and then he will be over here. Keep me informed, Stu."

As expected, within an hour, Jerry was arguing with Earl about entry into Graham's. Jerry recrossed the street, and Earl returned to the bar with Stu busy pumping gas. Taking a break from gas pumping, Stu realized that he couldn't see Jerry anymore, so he went hunting for him through the rooms of Graham's and the warehouse area. As he approached the back room, he saw Jerry ducking down as he came right through the back door riding Tony, his horse, with the dogs following. Startled, Stu shouted, "Jerry, get the hell out now!"

Jerry waved to Stu and continued on in with the dogs, who started to run all over. Some of the guests were scared to death, but others enjoyed the show.

Some of the people thought it would be fun to feed the dogs until they started eating the plastic plates and forks in one bite. Two dogs got into a fight, and luckily everyone had the sense to stay out of it. Jerry slowly walked Tony to the front door, bent down, and continued on down the boardwalk to the street. He gave one whistle to the dogs, and they all headed home.

Earl took Stu aside, "I thought I told you to keep an eye on that crazy bastard; now see what he did?" Stu stood there shaking his head. Earl added, "Ok, go get the flat shovel and scoop that horse shit out."

**JERRY BOURN RIDING
CHARLIE'S HORSE PINTO
(C. Kvistad)**

PACK TRAIN ABOUT TO LEAVE GLACIER FOR THE LONE JACK
(J. Steiner)

JERRY BOURN IN THE CABIN AS A YOUNG MAN
(D. Hamilton)

Year Number Three

JERRY'S HOSPITAL VISIT

Jerry Bourn was not welcome most of the time in either of the watering holes. When he came down from the mountains, his main goal was to drink, but most of the time he had no money. One or two of the Boys would buy him a drink or two and then he was on his way.

Later in the evening Jerry would walk around the bar and when he saw someone leave their stool, Jerry would quickly walk over to it. If the glass had anything left, Jerry would gulp it down, without setting it down, but if it was a full one, he would hop on the stool and sit there. Most of the time, with one look at dirty Jerry, anyone who purchased a drink would find another stool away from him. Earl found a solution to the Jerry-created problem by pouring all unfinished drinks, wine and beer, in a gallon jug and that became Jerry's standard drink.

One Saturday night in the middle of winter, Jerry was in Graham's with a large number of skiers, both Canadian and U.S. Jerry was drinking "Jerry's Drink" and he was behaving himself and having a great time. A skier gave him a small plate of BBQ ribs. All of a sudden, he made a sound and collapsed off the bar stool to the floor. Doug, the barkeep, came to take a look. "Something is wrong! I have seen Jerry drinking for years and tonight he was not drinking enough to pass out." Doug stood there looking, thinking that old Jerry might be dying.

A group of skiers went to Jerry's aid instantly. An emergency doctor, three emergency room nurses, two paramedics, and two firemen had all been up skiing and had stopped for a beer on their way home. Their first thought was that he may have choked on a rib bone but soon realized that was not the problem, but maybe some kind of a heart attack. A call went to 911 and the ambulance was dispatched from Bellingham. This group of emergency medical personnel worked on Jerry for 45 minutes before the aid car arrived. Jerry was taken to the emergency room.

After two days in the hospital, Jerry decided it was time to go home but the staff, knowing that he should remain in the hospital, hid his clothing. Everyone on the staff of the hospital encouraged him to stay. But no, Jerry thought it was time to go. He only had a hospital gown, so he took the pants and shoes of the man that was sharing the room with him. He hitchhiked up the highway and when no ride could be found, he walked. Twelve hours later, with frostbitten feet, Jerry made it to the Charlie Anderson Cabin at Shuksan.

PAMP SHOOTING AT PAMP

Little Pamp was the 17-year-old nephew of Pamp Bottiger. Little Pamp

67

had lived his whole life in Glacier down on the Bottiger farm, with his grandmother Hazel. Big Pamp had been like a father to him and taught him many things about life in general. At a very young age, Little Pamp was taught how to work and particularly how to work in the woods. When he was in grade school, he would go to work with his uncles on Saturdays and was taught all the dangers of logging. His knowledge of logging and logging equipment was very comparable to a mature man by the time he was 15 years old.

Late one Saturday afternoon, Little Pamp and two of his friends were working on his car at the Bottiger Shop in Glacier. The boys had a big night planned in Bellingham that evening, and they were doing a few minor adjustments to the car. Pamp came by in the late afternoon and started giving the threesome hell. Little Pamp figured out right away that his uncle had been drinking heavily, and he knew to stay away from him when he was in that kind of mood. But it got to the point that he couldn't take the verbal abuse any longer, so Little Pamp told his uncle to go on home.

Stu and two of his friends were hanging out, walking the streets of Glacier. All of a sudden they could hear a rage going on and they went to investigate. As they came around the corner, they could see Little Pamp and his friends at the car with Pamp standing near them, swearing like hell and holding a 30-06 rifle.

"You little shit, you never had respect for anything I taught you. I wish I would've ignored you," shouted Big Pamp. Little Pamp, trying to ignore

him, told him to go on home and sleep it off. This really provoked Big Pamp.

Little Pamp decided it was time to leave Glacier and let his uncle cool off. He turned and hollered at his uncle "For Christ sake, Uncle, go sleep it off." With that Uncle Pamp raised the rifle and pointed at the boys in the car. Little Pamp shouted to his friends, "Let's get the hell out of here!"

Stu was standing about 100 feet away and couldn't believe what he was hearing and seeing. The car roared down the street, heading toward Bellingham, when all of a sudden Pamp raised the rifle and shot. Stu wondered was Pamp aiming to hit the car or was he so drunk he was just shooting in the air when he did hit the side of a house? This house belonged to Chuck Graham. His teenage daughter was standing in the upstairs window watching the whole escapade take place down on the street. After the one shot, Pamp turned slowly, muttering to himself, and returned to his house.

The next day, the young girl was going through her clothes in her closet and she determined that every one of her dresses, coats, and blouses had a 30-06 bullet hole right down the middle of them. When she reported her findings to her father, the father went calling on Pamp. Pamp, as you may have expected, was not in the mood for company and when he heard the story, he told the fellow to get the hell out of his yard.

Within an hour a deputy sheriff from Whatcom County came calling on Glacier. When Graham told him the story, the deputy arrested Pamp and told him he was taking him to jail. Because of previous reports of shootings by

Pamp, the Deputy went to Pamp's house and removed all of his guns and took them with them. Pamp requested that he make one telephone call before he left. He called his nephew, Little Pamp, down at his mother's house. He told little Pamp to go down to the Great Western Lumber Company and pick up his logging payment, then come to Bellingham to the Sheriff's Department and bail him out. Well, Little Pamp did as he was told. He went to the mill, then to the Sheriff's Department; however, his uncle had not yet arrived. The deputy had another call down in the town of Sumas, which needed attention before returning to the Sheriff's Department.

Pamp was assigned a court date and as the date neared, a conversation with his nephew was held to discuss the matter. They agreed that there was no hard feelings from little Pamp toward his uncle and that no harm had been done. The discussion centered on what they were going to say in court about the events. The two of them made up a satisfactory story and were ready to go to trial.

The day of the trial arrived, with both Pamps going to the courthouse together. The story that was told by both was that, yes, the rifle went off but it was strictly an accident, that big Pamp was out showing little Pamp his new rifle and it discharged. The judge, hearing the testimony, made a decision that it was strictly an accident and no penalty was assessed. He also said, however, that Pamp was obligated to pay for the young Graham girl's clothes and the value was set at $500. The two Pamps thanked the judge and returned to their car.

Suddenly Big Pamp remembered all of his guns. He returned to the court room, charged in on the judge, told him that the deputy sheriff had taken all of his guns to town, and demanded that they be returned. The judge agreed and had the deputy return the guns to Pamp's closet.

As said earlier, all law stops at the Warnick Bridge.

❧

SECOND HAND LION

Mrs. Haggard, the postmaster in Maple Falls, was sorting outgoing mail one Monday afternoon. In doing so she spotted a letter to a circus in Chicago and the return address was Pamp Bottiger of Glacier, Washington. Pamp was the son of her brother Frank and right away this correspondence grabbed her attention. She decided to open it up and investigate. She found that Pamp and his good friend, George Impero from Maple Falls, were going together to buy a second hand lion from this circus. They had enclosed the $20 and shipping was free. This was a little hard to believe and so she called her brother Frank and told him the whole story.

Frank questioned Pamp and got the answer. He and George loved to hunt and they thought it would be quite something if this lion were to escape here in Glacier. They then would be called upon to go out, hunt it down, and shoot it. They saw no harm in the activity because they figured the lion was old and probably didn't have any teeth and therefore wouldn't cause injury. Hazel Bottiger called Mrs. Impero by telephone and got a similar answer. All parties, after giving the whole idea a second thought, agreed

69

that it would be best to cancel the order for the old worn-out lion.

MT. BAKER MARATHON

Stu was waiting on his favorite bench to catch up with his new friend Frank. Earl had said that Frank Bottiger was one of the contestants in the 1911 Mt. Baker Marathon Race from Bellingham to the top of Mt. Baker and back.

Sitting there, Stu thought about Frank and how he could have ever been in the race to the top of Mt. Baker. Today, when he walked the streets of Glacier, he was completely hunched over, always looking down, and never looking up. His pace was so slow that in some cases you weren't sure that he was moving and many people were concerned about his crossing the busy Mt. Baker Highway. At one time, one would assume that he had a very deep, baritone voice, but today it was a very quiet, gentle voice.

In his research Stu had found that the name Harvey Haggard kept coming up. Stu knew that Frank had some connection to the Haggard's.

Sure enough, Frank arrived right at 9:00 AM heading for Graham's. "Say Frank," asked Stu.

Frank turned to see Stu. "Hello Kid. Are you still dreaming about Loretta Young from 'The Call?'" asked Frank.

"Yes sir, I am," answered Stu with a big smile on his face.

Frank started for Graham's front door and Stu quickly added, "Frank, I sure would appreciate if you would tell me about those marathon races up Mt. Baker."

Turning back, Frank said, "Yes,

I know more about them than any other person since I ran in one of the races. Harvey Haggard, who won the second race, is the younger brother of my brother-in-law, but I can't talk now because I have these shakes I get every morning. The only way to get them to stop is go have a big mug of coffee. I sure would be happy to tell you all about the race after that."

Stu said disappointedly, "Whenever you can find the time, I'm ready." Stu knew that would be the last that he would see him sober, because he knew the coffee drink was half coffee and half whiskey.

Stu went into the storage room to do one of his Saturday jobs, that being sorting out the empty beer bottles and replacing them in the empty cases. After about half an hour, he heard the worn out voice of Frank call out, "Say, say kid, you ready to hear a good story?"

After Frank scared away a couple of younger kids from the bench, he and Stu took it over. Stu felt honored because he was with the man Frank Bottiger. "Say Kid," Frank started out, "I ran one of those races; I think it was in 1919."

Stu stopped Frank right there, "Frank, the races were run in 1911, 1912, and 1913; not in 1919."

Frank looked at him, "Who the hell is telling this, you or me? I'll check the year on the medal I won or ribbon-no, actually, I didn't get a damn thing."

Frank continued, "Well, the whole idea was the brain child of some crazy bastards of the Chamber of Commerce from Bellingham who called themselves the Mount Baker Club. This club was very supportive of outdoor activities in this area, but they were

PART OF THE BOYS OF GLACIER
From left: Leck Bottiger, his father Frank Bottiger, next two unknown, and Jake Steiner. (J. Steiner)

also very interested in the commercial development of the upper valley. The Club was promoting this whole Upper Nooksack Valley Area. This race was the first of their crazy ideas, then came the highway, and that was followed by the lodge. Now that lodge, I named it 'The Grand Lady of Mt. Baker.' It was something, I will tell you about that but not today.

"Now this Mount Baker Club came into town and built themselves a fine cabin right down there. Next, they raised money for trail construction with added monies from the Forest Service and Whatcom County. This group funded a number of trails; however, their first was the Mt. Baker Trail up Glacier Creek which was used for those damn races.

"This group of people had no idea the dangers of the mountain. These men knew nothing of the severity of the weather changes on the mountain.

LECK BOTTIGER ON THE LEFT–FRANK, HIS FATHER ON THE RIGHT
The two lived together for years in a small shack in town. (F. Bottiger)

One minute it could be clear, followed by a complete whiteout with heavy snow conditions. The runners on the mountain, within a few minutes, could be completely lost.

"When I ran the race, all the runners basically wore long, wool underwear with a pair of old cut off logging pants and nothing else. I wore a pair of my cork boots that I used for logging. You know that race almost got some fine young men killed up there. When I was running up the mountain, I got very tired and sat down. I began to sweat heavily, and then went into severe shivers. That was enough for me. I high-tailed it home. First place paid $500; not much to almost kill yourself.

"They had a series of judges spaced along the route and also on top. Charlie Bourn, ask him about it, he was a judge up on the mountain summit and he got his ass so cold he said, 'To hell with it,' and came home.

"There were two allowed routes for the race—one being the Glacier Route and the other the Heisler's Ranch Route outside of Deming. This trail went up the middle fork valley. The race started in Bellingham and finished in Bellingham. The runner had to come down from the top by the same route he took up. Now, each racer could use whatever means he wanted to get to Glacier and back to Bellingham. The same applied to the Heisler Route.

"The guys going the Glacier Route used the B.B. & B.C. Railroad for transportation. The train was a special three-unit train just for this purpose. The train remained in Glacier until the runners returned from the top. Once the first runner returned, the train would allow five minutes for the next runners and if none arrived, the train would take off out of Glacier, leaving the others behind.

"The Heisler Route runners used those damn race cars mainly provided by the Diehl Ford Company. The race was always the latter part of July, and it started at 11:00 PM. Yes, at night. Another thing that pissed me off was that you had to pay a $10 entrance fee —now in those days that was a hell of a lot of money.

"This was a big thing to Bellingham and Whatcom County. There were motor boat races on Lake Whatcom, baseball games, balloon rides, parachute jumps, the Sells-Floto Circus, and a parade on the day of the race.

"A hut, constructed at the summit of wire and canvas was used by the judges and provided shelter for racers to rest. After the races, it was left there for future mountain climbers to use. Stupid bastards, the next strong wind blew it to Canada. These people in Bellingham had no smarts about the conditions on that mountain. Almost every year of that damn race you couldn't see the top."

"Well," Frank started in again, "those rule makers in Bellingham created a complete set of rules. I remember the rules quite well, and I actually saw my copy just recently. They were named Marathon Contestant Pledge Honor, and each contestant had to abide by the rules. Now before the race was to begin, each runner had to sign the pledge and pay his $10 entry fee. I think the year that I raced there were about 10 runners—about half of the runners went the Glacier Route and the others by the Deming Route. Each runner was required to carry a flashlight for use during the night on Baker.

"At 11 PM, the cars went streaming down the street heading toward the mountain and the big old locomotive steamed away to Glacier. There were thousands of people at the starting point and within a matter of a few minutes they had all gone home to bed. The runners on the train had nothing to do but wait until they arrived in Glacier; however, the ones in the hopped up race cars had to bundle up to keep warm in the night air."

Frank continued, "The judges were stationed at timberline near the top, ready to check racers that got that far. I think there were about 15 additional guards that were stationed at intervals along the two trails to discourage cheating. The number of runners was considerably reduced by the time they reached the glaciers. All that remained in 1911 was six runners.

"Very suddenly, a cold wind came up, and the judges on the top were having a terrible time of it. The first five racers registered at the summit and then the wind forced the judges down to the crater rim.

"Those crazy people in Bellingham planned to have the judges carry a quantity of red firepower to the dome of Baker and this would be ignited at the time that the lead racer passed that point. They assumed that the people in town would be able to see the red

FRANK BOTTIGER AFTER A HARD NIGHT
Frank getting himself together in the morning. Note what he is sitting on and the bottle to his right. (J. Steiner)

73

THE GRAND LADY OF MT. BAKER
The Mt. Baker Lodge opened in 1927 and burned down in 1931. (Bert Huntoon Photo-Whatcom Museum, Bellingham, WA)

light from the top of Baker. The Pacific Telephone and Telegram Company ran a telephone line almost totally to the top of the mountain. They had planned that there could be communications from the top to Bellingham and that this would prove the efficiency of telephones. I do not remember if the phones worked at all. Lars Rye, yes, old Lars down at the river, was also a judge and he was positioned at the crater rim. His responsibility was with the telephone, and he was to identify runners coming and going in front of his location.

"The first runner to the top was Randall from the Glacier Route, with Harvey Haggard minutes behind. Joe Galbraith was first to reach the judges by the Deming Trail Route. In no time flat, Harvey passed Randall on the downward run and assumed the lead. By the time he reached Glacier, he was 5 to 10 minutes ahead. The train was

supposed to wait a few minutes for a second runner, but it took off toward Bellingham after just a couple minutes. Once aboard the train, Harvey wrapped himself in wool blankets to regain his body heat.

"The train, going like a bat out of hell, came around a curve and in the middle of the tracks was a big black bull weighing over a ton. You guessed it. The train engineer said that when the bull saw the approaching train it lowered its head and charged. The collision killed the bull instantly and derailed the train. No one on the train was injured but now Harvey had a problem of how to get back to Bellingham. The railroad people aboard tapped into the telephone line and requested a second locomotive, but the answer was that it would take too long.

"With 30 miles to go, Harvey flagged down a buggy on the road nearby, and with the driver, they took off toward

COMPLETION OF THE MOUNT BAKER CLUB IN GLACIER
The Mount Baker Club was instrumental in helping the development of the upper Nooksack Valley and the creation of the Mt. Baker Marathon. They very much wanted to see the upper valley developed economically and recreation wise. (Mount Baker Club, CPNWS, Western Washington University, Bellingham, WA)

Bellingham. However, after about half an hour, the old horse gave out and stopped. A rider on a horse came by next and told Harvey to take the horse, which he did. So Harvey took off again toward town. In the vicinity of Kendall, he fell off the horse and ended up in a big heap on the road bed. Picking himself up, Harvey flagged down a car, and he continued the trip to Bellingham. By the time he got there, he did not seem to have any serious injuries, but he was sure beat to hell.

"Harvey finally got to Bellingham after all of his troubles and upon his arrival he learned that he came in second place. Harvey went on to win the race in the second year, 1912.

"He went to work for the railroads over on the Peninsula and was involved in a serious accident when the boiler on the train exploded. He was injured very badly, and I don't know his current condition."

With a long pause from Frank who shuffled around on the seat, Stu assumed the history lesson was over. Stu said, "That was great, Frank. Old

**LARGE SIGN OVER MT. BAKER ROAD MARKING THE
START OF THE MT. BAKER TRAIL**

This large sign identified the start of the trail to the summit of Mt. Baker.
This was the actual starting point of the Mt. Baker Marathon races of 1911,
1912, and 1913. The large building to the right behind the power pole is the
Bellingham Bay & British Columbia railroad depot in Glacier. Beyond the
depot and to the left was the actual start of the trail leading to the summit.
(T. Warger)

**A SECOND SIGN MARKING THE ACTUAL START OF
THE MT. BAKER TRAIL**

Again, the actual start of the Mt. Baker Trail. When the actual contestants
started out, it was in the middle of the night and pitch dark. (T. Warger)

**ONE OF THE CONTESTANTS DISCUSSING A RULE
WITH A GROUP OF JUDGES**
**The building that they are standing in front of is the Mountain Home Hotel.
Next, down the street is the Bottiger-Haggard Store, and next to it is the later
Graham Store. Down the street is the Hotel Glacier. (Wilbur Sandison Photo-
Whatcom Museum, Bellingham, WA)**

Harvey certainly had an unlucky day did he not?"

"No, the story doesn't end there," Frank continued, "I was just moving around to arrange my man parts. There's more to it, you got to hear it all."

Frank went on. "Now last year, when we had the cattle drive, you remember the big black bull that I told you to be careful around? Well the big black bull that derailed the train was his great grandfather. Yes, it was my bull and, yes, he was quite a ways from Glacier. Now personally, I don't believe in fences and I'm more of an open range cattleman. The damn trees are always blowing over and knocking down the fences, so it's just easier not to have any.

"When the train hit the bull, it was not easy to determine whose bull it really was, but I haven't seen mine since that day. With the bull kicking on the railroad bed, someone had the sense to go out and cut his throat. Well, that was real good thinking, because the next day they had a huge beef barbecue down in Deming. The bull was the main attraction of the barbecue. Some of the people in Deming took credit for the bull and also said that they had planned the collision between the bull and the train, but I don't believe any of that. I know it was my bull. I think that was the first time that I ever heard the term barbecue, and the event was attended by hundreds of people. The first, second,

**MT. BAKER MARATHON REFEREE CAMP
AT THE RIM OF THE CRATER**
**The date of this picture is not known, but the weather appears to be perfect for
the event. That would indicate that it definitely was not in 1912. (C. Jenkins)**

and third place runners were all present, and gave their accounts of the race. Many reporters and photographers were on site, and the pictures and stories of the barbecue circulated up and down the West Coast. As you can imagine, Harvey was pissed off at me for years and wouldn't talk to me."

Again, Frank stirred and Stu assumed the story was over but Frank began once more, " I think this story is about over, because I am certainly getting thirsty, but there is one more thing I should add. The 1912 Marathon was run without any major catastrophes. Oh, there were added rules and regulations, and most of those were for the safety and well-being of the runners, but I sure did not enter this race, or any others, for I had had enough in 1911.

"One of the first rule changes in 1913 was that the race was open to contestants from any place in the world. The first two races were only open to the three Northwest Washington counties. Now, as you can imagine this brought about a lot of bitching from the local racers as in their opinion the racers should be local. Their concern was not listened to and the new rule stood. Another problem was in the past two races there were some collisions and near collisions between the cars and the train leaving the starting line, so a rule change was that the cars were given a one minute head start. This time the judges would erect shelters on the summit and stay there the night of the race. Finally, gasoline powered speeders would be provided for the second, third, and fourth man down the Glacier Trail.

"To follow the runner's progress, it was decided to string a telephone line from Glacier, where it could be connected to the existing line to the summit of the mountain along the race course. Phones could be installed every two miles over the 14 mile line, and runners on the Glacier Trail could be monitored. No Deming Trail monitoring was planned. A line was run to Mazama Park along the trail on the Deming Route.

"The rule change brought forth three distance runners: one from San Francisco, one from Calgary, Canada and the third one from a place I don't remember.

"Now, the day of the race had been chosen and everything was in order. The day before race day, the three summit judges called over the Glacier Trail telephone to say that they were turning back. The complete mountain was in a raging storm, and their opinion was that the race must be called off. Conditions on the upper

TELEPHONE SIGN INDICATING THE LOCATION OF PHONE LINE They were determined that by placing a telephone cable to the summit of Mt. Baker that this would promote the usage of telephones. However, they fell short of reaching the goal and this picture indicates that they were somewhere near the base of the Roman Wall. (C. Kvistad)

mountain were terrible with over three feet of new snow.

"After much argument and debate, the race was rescheduled for a week later. With the delay, the number of runners dropped from 16 to 9. The race was again to start at 11 PM. At 4:30 in the morning, the first place runner appeared at the summit and he reported that he had been lost for an hour below the summit. When he reached the judges, he almost collapsed. They warmed him up with a cup of hot coffee before he wandered into the blue a few minutes later. Word was received that Harvey Haggard had collapsed in the upper area of the Roman wall. As the judges started for him, Haggard appeared. The judges wondered if he could continue the race, but he seemed to recover with some hot coffee, and he realized that the rest of the race was down hill. It's hard to believe but all the runners and the judges made it down off the mountain that day. I don't remember who won that year. If you need to know that, I'm sure you can find it in some newspapers or in something.

"The 1913 race seemed to be very similar to the 1912, but the rule makers had made the rules much more stringent and safety-oriented for the runners. They were required to have additional warm clothing. The big event in this race was with a runner by the name of Victor Galbraith. He was related to all those other Galbraith's from Acme. Coming down the mountain, Galbraith was in a group with three other runners and all of a sudden he found himself further and further behind. He tried a shortcut and in doing so fell 40 feet into a hidden

JUDGES' CAMP AT MAZAMA LAKE ON THE DEMING ROUTE
The extreme difficult weather that plagued the race in 1913 is not indicated in this photo. (T. Warger)

**BELLINGHAM BAY AND BRITISH COLUMBIA NUMBER THREE
DERAILED AFTER COLLISION WITH A ONE-TON BULL**
Number three was probably traveling at the highest rate of speed in its history, possibly 50 miles an hour. However, if it had been traveling at a lower speed and making the turn, it would've probably still hit the bull. (C. Kvistad)

BELLINGHAM BAY AND BRITISH COLUMBIA #3
DERAILED WEST OF GLACIER
Harvey Haggard is second from the left dressed in a bathrobe. Also note the man sitting on the tracks is on a phone trying to get a second train. (C. Kvistad)

crevasse. In the fall he broke no bones and landed on a snow bridge forty feet down. The area was big enough that he was able to stand up, slap his hands, and move around to stay reasonably warm. About five hours after falling into the dark void, he heard the shouts from his cousin Joe and a forest ranger. They quickly dropped him a rope and hauled him up. He was cold and bruised but none the worse for wear. It was a close call. The rule change requiring the extra warm clothes was a good one.

"With this near fatal accident and some of the other events that had taken place in 1912 and 1913, the Mt. Baker Club and the Bellingham Chamber of Commerce decided that they had had enough. It had been a great event for

the region, but the possibility of being responsible for someone's death was too great."

With that, Frank got up, pointed to the door, and headed in. Stu jumped up, caught up with him, and told him how much he appreciated all the information. That night in discussing the marathons with his mother, she was dumbfounded that Frank could recall the details that he did.

In later research, Stu determined that all of Frank's information was accurate. It turned out to be one of the best discussions that Stu had concerning the history of the area.

"Say Earl, where's the kid?" asked Frank.

Earl, looking up from his newspaper, answered, "Well, Frank, it is Tuesday,

THE REMAINS OF THE BULL
It would appear from this photo that it would've been difficult for Frank Bottiger to know for sure if this was his bull. Old number three did a great job of tenderizing the beef. (T. Warger)

**JOE GALBRAITH IN THE BETSY WITH
HUGH DIEHL AS THE DRIVER**
Note the condition of the road bed. Joe was actually behind Haggard by about 28 minutes in reaching the summit, but due to Haggard's bad luck he went on to win the race. (T. Warger)

**RACE CAR RETURNING TO BELLINGHAM
WITH RUNNER ABOARD**
**When the contestants returned to Bellingham, they were met by a very large
and joyous crowd. At this point, no one knew what had happened to Haggard
and the troubles he was having. (T. Warger)**

and it's the month of April; I believe the kid is in school."

Frank then continued, "Well, that does make sense, but I'm not sure that damn kid needs to go to school. He's already smarter than most people, particularly in this damn town. Here, give him this old newspaper that I found concerning the marathon race. I thought that my old lady had thrown them away, but damned if I didn't find this one. Now you tell him, again, that the train did not hit Loop's bull; it was my bull."

WINNER HARVEY HAGGARD'S 1912 FIRST PLACE MEDALLION
The mascot of all the marathon races was the mountain goat and the slogan that was used throughout "Goa-to-it". The lettering on the back of the medallion:
L W Thurston
In Appreciation of faithful service 1912
Harvey Haggard
14 K
(T. Warger)

**JOE GALBRAITH, WINNER OF THE
MT. BAKER MARATHON, 1911**
Joe's first place earned a cash prize of $500. Joe had won the race by going up
the Deming route. (T. Warger)

HARVEY HAGGARD CAME IN SECOND IN 1911 AND FIRST IN 1912
Harvey's second place finish earned him $250 in 1911. (T. Warger)

**THE HUGE BARBECUE WAS ATTENDED BY HUNDREDS
UNTIL THEY RAN OUT OF BULL**

The barbecue had not been scheduled; however, due to the provided beef it was added to the schedule. It was attended by hundreds of people. (C. Kvistad)

**FRANK BOTTIGER'S TRAIN-TENDERIZED
BEEF–FIT FOR THE BANQUET**

One can see in this photo, in 1913 people knew how to dress for a barbecue. (C. Kvistad)

**THE RESCUE PARTY RETURNING WITH VICTOR GALBRAITH
WHO FELL INTO A HIDDEN CREVASSE**

**Victor was a very fortunate fellow and surely would not have survived the
night. (T. Warger)**

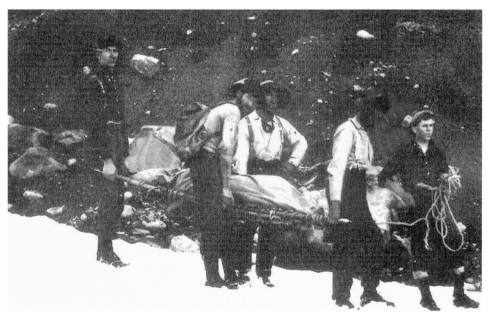

**VICTOR GALBRAITH BEING CARRIED AT THE POINT THAT
THE TRAIL CHANGED FROM SNOW TO ROCKS**

**The moving of someone in his condition down the mountain required a
tremendous effort by a group of people. (T. Warger)**

LAST EDITION

THE BELLINGHAM HERALD

ONLY BELLINGHAM EVENING NEWSPAPER WITH ASSOCIATED PRESS DISPATCHES

HERALD WANT ADS DO the WORK

COUNTY OFFICIAL PAPER. BELLINGHAM, WASHINGTON, FRIDAY, AUGUST 11, 1911. VOL. XXI. NO. 112.

Galbraith Says Rival Rode Horse

FAST MAN ON DEMING TRAIL

J. F. GALBRAITH
Winner of the Mount Baker race, and of The Herald trophy. Galbraith won the event in clean, sportsmanlike manner.

SENSATIONAL RACE IS TALK OF COUNTY

Indomitable Haggard, Champion of Glacier Trail Against Deming Contestants In Great Mountain Marathon, Is Tossed Naked About the Seats of a Wrecked Coach, Thrown From Bronco, Faints Twice In Rapidly-Moving Automobile and Yet Arrives Second at Destination—Galbraith's Chief Rival Proves Himself Plucky Winner.

FARMER IS CAUSE OF TRAIN WRECK

Twenty-Year-Old Packer Is Hero of Glacier, Maple Falls and Bellingham—Accident Does Not Detract From His Glory Although It Robbed Him of First Place.

By H. H. MATHESON.

Not yet has the County of Whatcom, the state, the whole Northwest recovered its equilibrium, the nervous tension beginning some hours before 10 o'clock Wednesday night when the greatest race in the history of the United States began—the Mt. Baker climb. Staid citizens who regard with indifference the struggles of the Giants, or the White Sox, and who look upon an approaching championship battle of heavyweights with no more perturbation than they do a missionary tea, Wednesday night ran about the streets like lunatics, shouting, cheering, trying to tell every body else what every body else was trying to tell at the same time.

Then when the autos and the special train whizzed away in the dark, everybody had nervous chills for something would happen, that this racer would fall by the wayside, or that something untoward would happen.

Something did happen, many things; and it is the happenings, accidents, the hazards of contest that makes competition keen and worth while, as it is differences of opinion that engender horse races.

Nothing can detract from the splendid victory scored by J. F. Galbraith, of Acme. His achievement was clean cut, decisive, and deserves the place in the history of the Northwest which it merits.

But the real race, with its moving accidents of flood, and field, and mountain fastness, was the race run by Harvey Haggard, the 20-year-old packer for the Polson Mine company, of Glacier, who plunged into the darkness of the trail at Glacier Wednesday night at 30 seconds past 11 o'clock, carrying an old fashioned miners "bug," a candle stuck in a two-pound lard pail, and who tore back through the woods the following morning on the dead run and scrambled aboard the B. B. & B. C. special at just two winks past 9 o'clock.

Haggard had not entered the coach when the train was under full speed, tearing down the steep grade and around the curves below Glacier at a speed that would stand one's hair on end.

Dr. E. O. Beebe, Tom Kelly and a number of others, stretched Haggard out on the cot, yanked off his clothes and began to rub him down.

At 7 minutes past 9 o'clock, with the train going terrifically, an 1,800 pound red bull, the property of Dan J. Loop, a rancher living near Glacier, burst from the thick underbrush alongside the track and planted his front feet in the middle of the track, a few feet ahead of the engine.

The engine had just time to emit a startled scream from its whistle, when the impact came.

The bull, flung high in the air, fell a distance ahead of the engine, was ground under the wheels, lifting the front trucks of the locomotive from the rails.

As if reluctant to leave the track, the engine and the special coach, both now derailed, ploughed along for ten rods, tearing up the iron, and cutting deep groves in the brand new ties.

Then came a terrific crash, the engine and the tender telescoped, the coach stood on end, fell back, turned over.

Haggard, lying on the bunk as naked as the day he was born, hit the ceiling of the coach, was slammed into a corner and bounced back among the seats.

A whole lot of three cushion caroms were executed by that coach, and the fourteen passengers aboard the special received multitudinous bumps and bruises, but miraculously, no one was badly injured.

The bunch scrambled to the top side of the car, fished Haggard out of the mess, and sat him down upon a railroad tie. A blanket was wrapped about him, and then some one happened to think that it might be a good idea to dress him.

His trousers and a sweater were pulled onto him, and he was stood up for inspection.

"I am all right," said Haggard simply, "but I am afraid I've lost the race."

A man driving with a horse and buggy was hailed, Haggard was load-

(Continued on Page Four.)

ENGINEER JOHN GOLITHON
Who was found hanging to the throttle when engine No. 3 went into the ditch.

WAITING FOR HAZARD TO APPEAR DOWN TRAIL—SHOT HAS BEEN FIRED ADVISING GLACIER PEOPLE THAT RUNNER IS WITHIN QUARTER OF A MILE OF TRAIN.

THREE THOUSAND CROWD INTO PIONEER PARK

Biggest Gathering In History of Whatcom County Pioneer's Association Fills Park at Ferndale On Second Day of Annual Celebration—Every Train Is Loaded to Guards and Scores Cannot Get Aboard—Wagons, Autos, Stages Bring Huge Crowds.

ANNUAL ORATION IS DELIVERED BY REVELLE

Enlarged Park Gives Plenty of Room for Pioneers and Visitors—Lummi Indians Repeat Tribal Dances—Pioneer Poem Read This Afternoon—Loving Cup Presentation Tomorrow.

(Staff Correspondence.)

Ferndale, Aug. 11.—Crowded to the limit with the biggest assemblage of pioneers and visitors ever gathered to celebrate Pioneers' day here, the big park where the pioneers picinc is being held today presents a scene which sends the memories of the old-timer back to generations gone when the Nooksack valley was a wilderness. Three thousand people are crowded into the grounds and everyone is having a good time. Every train was loaded to the guards and scores at station after station could not get aboard. Wagons, buggies, autos and stages are dumping their loads every minute and the huge crowd is being swelled every hour. This is the big day, marked as it is by the pioneer oration by Thomas Revelle, of Seattle, the address of welcome by George Ellsperman, of Blaine, and the reply by Loomis Baldry, of Bellingham. The address of welcome will be delivered at 3 o'clock and the other events on the program will follow close. The first part of the day has been spent by the pioneers and visitors in renewing old acquaintanceship and making new friendships.

There were a few athletic events run off this forenoon.

Today's program in full follows: Afternoon—Special literary and memorial program at 3 o'clock; York's band, of Bellingham; address of welcome by George A. Ellsperman, of Blaine; response on behalf of guests

(Continued on Page Three.)

HORSES ARE HIDDEN ALONG TRAIL

Galbraith, Winner of Race to Top of Mt. Baker and Return Over Deming Trail, Files Remonstrance With Contest Committee In Which He Claims He Saw Two Saddle Horses Hidden Alongside the Trail—Other Evidence Is In Hands of Committee Which Leads to Belief That One Contestant Used Horse for Part of Distance—All Guards Will Be Called In to Testify.

HAGGARD FIRST TO REACH SUMMIT

Belief Prevails That Galbraith Made Best Time On Deming Trail but No Statement Can Be Issued Until Judges Confer With Contest Committee.

Official time of the arrival of the four contestants—Haggard, Galbraith, Magnussen and Riddle,—as shown by the credentials signed by the judges on top of the mountain and as again checked and countersigned by the contest committee, show the following:

Haggard	5:18 a. m.
Galbraith	5:37 a. m.
Magnussen	5:46 a. m.
Turner Riddle	6:46 a. m.

According to the story told by Riddle a storm enveloped the top of the mountain when he arrived near the summit. The judges, Riddle claims, had returned a short distance down the crater for shelter and, instead of permitting him, Riddle, to continue to the top, handicapped him forty minutes and sent him back on the down trip.

If these facts are borne out by the word of the judges, who are expected to arrive in the city some time this evening, Riddle's time to the point where the judges met him was 6:06.

The statement that Norman Randle was the first to reach the summit of the mountain is declared by Haggard to be a mistake. Haggard claims to have been the first to reach the summit, and the official credential slip bears him out.

By the official credential slip Haggard beat every other contestant to the top by nineteen minutes.

Galbraith filed a remonstrance with the contest committee, claiming that he saw two saddle horses hidden alongside the trail. Other evidence is in the hands of the committee which leads to the belief that one contestant used a horse for a distance over the Deming trail.

All guards stationed along the trail, the judges who were on the summit, and, it is understood, a rancher of the region, will be called into a closed session to decide whether the record of one contestant shall be allowed to stand.

There is not the slightest doubt in the mind of anyone that Galbraith won his splendid victory on the square. On the other hand, the statement made that another contestant made the fastest time is disputed by the committee. There appears to be no doubt that Haggard made the fastest time to the summit and return to Glacier, but no definite statements regarding this feature of the race, or any other, is available until the contest committee confers with the judges.

The contest committee thus far makes this official statement and none other.

Galbraith won the first prize, with Haggard second.

The feature of the race on the Deming trail was the spectacular and wonderful run made by Hugh Diehl, of Diehl & Simpson, in the old Ford car "Betsy," carrying the winner, Galbraith.

"Betsy" is the work car used by the Diehl & Simpson company for carrying supplies, and is of a model two or three years old. "Betsy" has the speed bug, however, and no amount of trucking or other menial employment has ever sufficed to reduce this old girl to anything like a sedate deportment.

When the Diehl & Simpson company was approached by the Deming people to produce a fast automobile to convey a racer to the trail, Hugh Diehl ran his eye over the trim, neat, new cars backed up against the walls of the garage and finally permitted his gaze to rest lovingly on "Betsy."

"We have got just exactly the wagon for that stunt," replied Mr. Diehl, pointing to the old gray work car.

"You don't mean that delivery cart with the tin can on the rear, do you," was asked.

"We do," was Diehl's somewhat spirited answer.

So the boys in the garage turned to and fitted "Betsy" out with some new racing shoes and removed all the ruffles and stays and divested her of her hobble skirt with the mud guard ornaments, patted the old lady on the back and lined her up in front of the

(Continued on Page Three.)

FAST MAN ON GLACIER TRAIL

HARVEY HAGGARD
Winner of second prize, whose race was rendered spectacular by three successive wrecks.

DELEGATES ARE ENTERTAINED BY VISIT TO LAKE

Silver Beach Civic Club Is Host to Delegates to Third Annual Convention of Western Federation of Civic Improvement Clubs—Vessel Is Chartered and Beauties of Lake Whatcom Shown, Lunch Being Served at White City Hotel—L. C. Short Presides Over Afternoon Session.

RUFUS WILSON SPEAKS ON COOPERATIVE WORK

Address of Welcome Is Delivered by Mayor J. P. de Mattos, While Response Is Made by President William Crehan, of Tacoma—Henry Engberg Delivers Most Interesting Address On Mt. Baker.

This morning between seventy-five and one hundred delegates to the third annual convention of the Western Federation of Civic Improvement Clubs, which opened in Bellingham yesterday, are the guests of the Silver Beach Civic club and were entertained with a boat ride on Lake Whatcom. Returning from this about noon, luncheon was served to the delegates at the White City hotel at 1 o'clock.

The afternoon session convened about 2 o'clock with President L. C. Short, of the Silver Beach Civic club, presiding. Features of the session were an address on "The Mutual Advantages of Washington," by former Governor Albert E. Mead; an address on "Parks and Playgrounds," by Secretary L. H. Weir, of the National Playground association, and an ad-

(Continued on Page Six.)

PERKINS SAYS PUBLICITY WILL CURE EVILS

New York Financier and Steel Trust Director Says Government Commission Should Be Appointed to Focus Limelight of Publicity On Operations of Corporations and Trusts and Evils Will Be Abolished.

INDUSTRIAL SITUATION MAY BE INVESTIGATED

Congressman Littleton Announces Intention of Introducing Resolution Providing for Commission to Make Drastic Investigation of Industrial Conditions and Find Cure.

Washington, D. C., Aug. 11.—George W. Perkins, the New York financier, suggested to the house steel corporation committee of inquiry today that a government commission which would insure focusing the limelight of publicity on the business affairs of great corporations would do much to eradicate present-day trust evils and preserve their virtues.

Following Perkins' suggestion, Representative Littleton, of New York, announced that a resolution soon would be introduced in congress providing for a thorough investigation of the industrial situation of the country.

"I am advised," Mr. Littleton said, "that there is to be a thorough inquiry into the commercial ills of the nation, and that a conference will be called to determine the problem of how to deal with the industrial situation in America. It is a project that will involve a most drastic investigation and bring together capital and

(Continued on Page Six.)

FOUR SHOT TO DEATH IN COURT ROOM

Man Arrested for Shooting On Street, Opens Fire As Court Orders Him to Jail—Judge Shot to Death, Marshal Killed, While Deputy Kills Slayer.

FIFTH FATALLY HURT

While Riot Was Occurring Father of Prisoner Falls Out of Second Story Window and Is Fatally Hurt.

(Associated Press by Leased Wire.)

Denton, Ill., Aug. 11.—Attempting to escape after being remanded to jail for examination, Martin Shadowens today shot Justice of the Peace James Mannon, City Marshal John Stakinrider and a spectator and cut Deputy Tom Mackey. Mackey shot and killed Shadowens, whose father, Charles, fell from a second-story window and was probably fatally hurt. The shooting occurred at Christopher, near here, at midnight.

The Shadowens had been arrested for shooting on the streets after a man named Denges had been injured by a bullet. Martin Shadowens pleaded to be allowed to appear in the justice court today, but Justice Mannon ordered that he be taken to jail.

Without warning Martin shot the justice through the right arm and then put three bullets through the body of John Stakrider, who may die. The courtroom was crowded with spectators. William Schultz received a bullet intended for Mackey.

Mackey was injured in approaching Shadowens before he fired the fatal shot. In the excitement Charles Shadowens fell from the courtroom window on the second floor.

The lawyers and the real estate men play ball tomorrow afternoon at the fair grounds at 3 o'clock for the benefit of the Mount Baker club.

COMPROMISE IS REACHED ON WOOL

Full Conference Committee Reaches Compromise and Bill Carries Impost of 29 Per Cent On All Raw Wool—Classifications Are Abolished.

MEETING OPEN TO PRESS

For First Time In History of Government Conference Is Thrown Open to Press—Taft Expected to Veto Measure.

(Associated Press by Leased Wire.)

Washington, D. C., Aug. 11.—The full house and senate conference committee on the wool tariff revision bill today agreed on a flat rate of 29 per cent., on raw wool. The committee also agreed on the house classification of wool. The agreement on these two points seemed to remove the greatest obstacles in the way of final agreement, which, it was said, might be reached.

There was apparently a determination to force an early agreement on the wool measure. Threats to postpone the present session indefinitely if an agreement was not reached were freely made. The free list bill, it was said, was receiving comparatively little attention, many senators and representatives insisting that it be subordinated to wool.

It was learned that Representative Underwood and Senator LaFollette, the sub-committee on conference, had been only 2½ cents apart on raw wool. Mr. Underwood held out for a duty of 27½ per cent. ad valorem, while LaFollette insisted on 30 per cent. The full committee compromised on 29 per cent.

As agreed on, the classification provision of the bill reads:

"On wool of the sheep, hair of the camel, goat, alpaca and other like animals, and on all wools and hair on the skin of such animals, the duty shall be 29 per cent. ad valorem."

The LaFollette bill called for two classes of wool—wool and hair on the skin being in a second class—whereas the house provision, accepted by

(Continued on Page Six.)

PASSENGERS OF SPECIAL JUST A FEW SECONDS AFTER THE WRECK HAD OCCURRED.

ENGINE NO. 3 OF THE B. B. & B. C. SPECIAL AS SHE LAY ON HER SIDE.

SENSATIONAL RACE IS TALK OF COUNTY

Indomitable Haggard, Champion of Glacier Trail Against Deming Contestants In Great Mountain Marathon, Is Tossed Naked About the Seats of a Wrecked Coach, Thrown From Bronco, Faints Twice In Rapidly-Moving Automobile and Yet Arrives Second at Destination—Galbraith's Chief Rival Proves Himself Plucky Winner.

FARMER IS CAUSE OF TRAIN WRECK

Twenty-Year-Old Packer Is Hero of Glacier, Maple Falls and Bellingham—Accident Does Not Detract From His Glory Although It Robbed Him of First Place.

By H. H. MATHESON.

Not yet has the County of Whatcom, the state, the whole Northwest recovered its equilibrium, the nervous tension beginning some hours before 10 o'clock Wednesday night when the greatest race in the history of the United States began—the Mt. Baker climb. Staid citizens who regard with indifference the struggles of the Giants, or the White Sox, and who look upon an approaching championship battle of heavyweights with no more perturbation than they do a missionary tea, Wednesday night ran about the streets like lunatics, shouting, cheering, trying to tell every body else what every body else was trying to tell at the same time.

Then when the autos and the special train whizzed away in the dark, everybody had nervous chills for something would happen, that this racer would fall by the wayside, or that something untoward would happen.

Something did happen, many things; and it is the happenings, accidents, the hazards of contest that makes competition keen and worth while, as it is differences of opinion that engender horse races.

Nothing can detract from the splendid victory scored by J. F. Galbraith, of Acme. His achievement was clean cut, decisive, and deserves the place in the history of the Northwest which it merits.

But the real race, with its moving accidents of flood, and field, and mountain fastness, was the race run by Harvey Haggard, the 20-year-old packer for the Polson Mine company, of Glacier, who plunged into the darkness of the trail at Glacier Wednesday night at 30 seconds past 11 o'clock, carrying an old fashioned miners "bug," a candle stuck in a two-pound lard pail, and who tore back through the woods the following morning on the dead run and scrambled aboard the B. B. & B. C. special at just two winks past 9 o'clock.

Haggard had not entered the coach when the train was under full speed, tearing down the steep grade and around the curves below Glacier at a speed that would stand one's hair on end.

Dr. E. O. Beebe, Tom Kelly and a number of others, stretched Haggard out on the cot, yanked off his clothes and began to rub him down.

At 7 minutes past 9 o'clock, with the train going terrifically, an 1,800 pound red bull, the property of Dan J. Loop, a rancher living near Glacier, burst from the thick underbrush alongside the track and planted his front feet in the middle of the track, a few feet ahead of the engine.

The engine had just time to emit a startled scream from its whistle, when the impact came.

The bull, flung high in the air, fell a distance ahead of the engine, was ground under the wheels, lifting the front trucks of the locomotive from the rails.

As if reluctant to leave the track, the engine and the special coach, both now derailed, ploughed along for ten rods, tearing up the iron, and cutting deep groves in the brand new ties.

Then came a terrific crash, the engine and the tender telescoped, the coach stood on end, fell back, turned over.

Haggard, lying on the bunk as naked as the day he was born, hit the ceiling of the coach, was slammed into a corner and bounced back among the seats.

A whole lot of three cushion caroms were executed by that coach, and the fourteen passengers aboard the special received multitudinous bumps and bruises, but miraculously, no one was badly injured.

The bunch scrambled to the top side of the car, fished Haggard out of the mess, and sat him down upon a railroad tie. A blanket was wrapped above him, and then some one happened to think that it might be a good idea to dress him.

His trousers and a sweater were pulled onto him, and he was stood up for inspection.

"I am all right," said Haggard simply, "but I am afraid I've lost the race."

A man driving with a horse and buggy was hailed, Haggard was load-

(Continued on Page Four.)

SENSATIONAL RACE IS TALK OF COUNTY

(Continued From Page One.)

ed in, and the man lashed his steed into a dead run. The emergency phone had been hooked over the company telephone line, and the message sent in to Maple Falls to have the auto ready.

The automobile had previously been stationed, by agreement, at Kendall crossing, and so a saddle horse was got ready to carry the plucky racer to the machine.

Joe Bowlner's Buster horse, one of these nervous cayuses with feet and legs like a deer, and an eye that shows all the white, stood saddled at the Maple Falls crossing. Willing hands lifted Haggard from the rig, and placed him on Buster's back.

Then Buster just naturally frittered the landscape away behind him until, as Haggard describes it, the scenery looked like a moving picture film running amuck.

Buster made a wonderful run to Kendall crossing, but when he saw that an automobile was stationed there and that he was not to have the honor of carrying the doughty racer into Bellingham, he planted both front feet and shot Haggard off over his head.

Auto Driver Harry Lewis picked Haggard up, placed him in the car and the wild race for Bellingham began. Twice on the way to town Haggard fainted, but finished second in the manner now known to everybody who has been following the race.

In reply to the many questions as to how the automobile happened to be at Kendall crossing, it may be explained that the Glacier people had provided the means for bringing in the racer on the Glacier trail who arrived second.

The second racer down on the Glacier trail was to be carried on the speeder to Kendall and loaded into a waiting automobile. It was this waiting machine that conveyed Haggard into the city.

The incidents of the wreck are many, each person having a separate and distinct list of impressions to relate.

As soon as the car had piled up the hiss of steam advised the passengers in the coach that trouble might exist about the engine and tender.

The engine lay upon its side; Engineer John Golithon, good engineer that he is, was in his cab, shutting off the steam, and ready at his post to do anything that it was possible to do to avert further untoward results.

Fireman Albert Graaseland was shot out of the cab to the side of the track, and was uninjured, as was the engineer.

Fireman Helper Paul Wenning suffered the most and possibly the only hurt experienced by any man on the train.

When the engine and the tender telescoped Wenning's feet were caught in the mass of splintered wood. Pinned as tightly as if locked into stocks, Wenning was unable to move. The scalding steam was pouring up all about him, the feed pipe from the oil tank was spouting beside him.

The first thought was to protect him from burns, the second to free him before the oil might catch fire.

Under the direction of Dr. E. O. Beebe, of Everson, who was on board the special as medical aid for the racers, blankets were wrapped about Wenning's feet and legs. Then the bunch turned to and gathered ferns by the arm full. These green plants were packed in solidly all about Wennig's body, and he was protected perfectly against the scalding steam.

Then the emergency kit of tools was tapped, saws and hammers gotten out and the imprisoned helper hacked free.

Tom Kelly, the Bellingham wrestler who was one of the contestants, but who quit at the coal camp on the up trip and returned to Glacier, furnished a lot of amusement for the Glacier folks and incidentally a boost for the hikers of that city when he exclaimed in explanation of why he had dropped out of the race:

"I have seen trained fleas, jack rabbits, antelopes, giraffes and mountain sheep, but these Glacier hikers beat any of them. Not for my money! You get me into no race with mountain goats."

In passing, and to do the man justice, Kelly is a sportsman through and through. He was the first to stick forth a hand to help Haggard onto the special, worked like a beaver to rub Haggard down, and when the wreck occurred, dove through a window and brought the naked and tired racer out onto solid earth.

Kelly never ceases to extol the wonderful race made by Haggard, is a strong puller for the Glacier trail; and is mentioned by the people of Glacier in the colloquial "Has anybody here seen Kelly?" with genuine affection and respect.

Honors have not yet ceased for Haggard. Beside the $50 purse, a collection amounting to $30 was presented to him in the Chamber of Commerce last night. Glacier and Maple Falls have made up an additional purse of $100, the citizens of Maple Falls have arranged a banquet in his honor for Wednesday night, and he has been elected, not mayor, but king of Glacier, and the lands that there adjacent lie.

The track was cleared at the scene of the wreck last night, and the afternoon Glacier train permitted to pass. The engine will be lifted sometime today. The whole damage to the engine and car consists of some broken pipes.

the smashing of the front platform of the coach and a few broken windows.

When the train pulled out Wednesday night the watches of Dr. Beebe, Passenger Agent Somers, Joe Anderson, photographer, sent by Henry Engberg, and The Herald representative were set together.

The run to Noon station, seven miles distant, was made from a dead stop, in 7 minutes, 20 seconds. The fastest time made on the up trip was from Clearbrook to Sumas, a distance of three miles, made in 2 minutes flat. The run from Bellingham to Glacier, from a dead stop, a full stop at the Northern Pacific crossing, and a slowing up for one or two sharp curves, was made in exactly 60 minutes.

The feeling at Glacier and at Maple Falls is intense against Loop, the owner of the bull that derailed the special. Despite the fact that every farmer in the district was asked to keep in his stock, the request being made for the good of the Glacier trail project, and not for any individual, Loop released seven head of stock, one of which endangered the lives of seventeen people, cost the railroad company money, and undoubtedly defeated Haggard from winning first place in the greatest race ever won. If Loop can reconcile himself to the situation, if he can elicit any grains of selfish satisfaction out of the outcome, the people of Glacier, Maple Malls, of Bellingham, of the whole county and state, wish him joy. You are a good sport, Mr. Loop, we are glad we met you.

Bellingham Herald August 11, 1911_e
CPNWS Newspaper Collection
Center for Pacific Northwest Studies
Heritage Resources
Western Washington University
Bellingham, WA 98225-9123

Year Number Four

BOTTIGER VS MARR

Stu stood on the Graham's boardwalk with a group of people. The fight had occurred across the street in Hestle's Mt. Baker Inn. The argument started with Jerry Marr in front of Graham's and Pamp Bottiger in front of The Inn. Jerry had gotten off the crew bus from plowing snow at the ski area and Pamp, seeing him from across the street, started shouting at him. Jerry was not about to take any verbal abuse and went directly across the street. Instantly the two were in a shoving match and Jerry decided to forget it, so he turned to cross the street. The two were standing at a tire changing station and Pamp saw a large ball pin hammer. He quickly grabbed the hammer and went after Jerry. Pamp hit Jerry a glancing blow. If it had been straight on Jerry would have been killed. He turned, grabbed hold of Pamp struggling to stay conscious and, forced Pamp back into a small storage room.

Jerry gave Pamp a terrible beating

STEINER'S HOMESTEAD CABIN
Herman Steiner with his wife Lena and their first son in 1895 on their 160 acre farm on the upper Nooksack River. (J. Steiner)

and left the room with Pamp on the floor, unconscious. An ambulance was called from Bellingham and it took a full hour to reach Glacier. Pamp spent two weeks in the hospital with broken ribs and fractured bones in his face.

After the fight, everyone left the site and went home, Stu couldn't wait to get home and tell Liz. It took two days for Stu to corner Earl Graham and ask for the whole story of Bottiger vs Marr.

A few days later, the two sat down on the boardwalk bench and Earl started the story, "Have you been taught in history class about the Hatfield's and the McCoy's family feud? We have here the Glacier version of that feud. The Bottiger Family first hit Glacier in about 1904 with Frank operating the Haggard-Bottiger Store. Over a period of time, Frank and his two sons became a very dominating family here and somewhat ruled the town. Oh, nothing real bad, just that the point was always made.

"The Marr family settled in the mid 1940's here in Glacier and then down to an existing farm that adjoined the Bottiger Farm. The Marr family consisted of four boys and one girl, Bonnie. Now, Sque Marr was a strong-willed man, and he taught his sons to stand up for their rights.

"The hard feelings started like almost any other disagreement over almost nothing. The Marrs had said that they would provide help to the Bottigers in putting in their annual hay crop. Well, the day it was to happen, the Marrs got mixed up and went to the Steiner farm to hay. This was what started it.

"By this time, Pamp was running the Bottiger Farm as Frank had moved up town. One day, Pamp decided that he needed to dig a ditch along the common property line but instead of digging it he decided to place a line of dynamite charges and blast the ditch. In a logger's mind if a little dynamite would work why not double it? In setting off the charge, it blew all the pictures off the Marr house walls and broke all of Mrs. Marr's good china in the china cabinet.

"Next, Mrs. Marr discovered she was losing chickens from her chicken house and couldn't see any indication that any wild animal was getting to them. One day, she discovered she was missing two roosters. She found a tube of lipstick in the hen house. Mrs. Marr, with lipstick in hand, headed down to the Bottiger farm house to discuss it with Mrs. Bottiger. She asked if Janet, the daughter of Mrs. Bottiger, had lost her lipstick and Mrs. Bottiger replied, 'yes.'

"In returning the tube of lipstick, she said, 'Keep the hell away from my hen house.'

"The Marr kids had to ride their bikes or walk past the Bottiger farm house to get to Glacier. They felt that the Bottiger dogs were trained to chase only them. If you were riding past the house, this pack of five to six wolves would chase them for at least a mile. All the Marr kids learned to ride their bikes with one foot on the handle bars.

"They would sneak down and fish in the creek that ran through the Bottiger field. On one occasion, the Bottigers saw them and started to chase after them. The littlest Marr boy had caught a fine fish and with the fish, he headed home running as hard as he could, but the fish hook caught him in the leg. He made it home with the fish and the fish hook buried in his leg.

"There was one more incident that really put the frosting on the cake. In 1952, the Marrs started a mink farm to raise and harvest the pelts. Now farmed mink are very excitable, with a sudden scare or noise the female will abort their unborn offspring. Not knowing if this incident was intentional or not, but Pamp decided to blast out a dozen of old growth stumps near the property line. Well, the sudden noise and the shaking of the ground made over half of the female mink abort. This seemed to be the last straw.

"Jerry, the oldest Marr son, went into the service upon graduation from high school. He was a very muscular young man, and the military service had filled him out even more. Jerry had done a little boxing in the service.

"Upon his return, he went to Graham's one night to have a beer and see all of his old friends. Well, Pamp was present and was in a somewhat drunken condition. In no time Pamp started to bad mouth young Marr, and Jerry could only take so much. Finally he jumped off his barstool, grabbed Pamp and hit him twice. Pamp was down and out for the count. With that incident I would have thought that Pamp would keep his mouth shut but he didn't."

MT. BAKER AVALANCHE

William Parke, the Glacier Forest Service District Ranger, was sitting in his living room at eight o'clock on a Saturday night in July. There was a knock on his front door and upon investigating he found two young people, a man and a woman, standing there. The girl excitedly stated, "We've had an accident and we need to report it." Bill looked outside expecting to see a car with damage on it but not seeing that he turned back to the two. Any kind of an incident that occurred up in the National Forest was commonly reported to the District Ranger before the County Sheriff. The girl went on to explain, "There was a snow slide up on Mt. Baker this afternoon and six of our party are missing."

The two gave Bill the whole report. They were part of the Western Washington College annual mountain climbing trip up Mt. Baker. The trip had gone as per plan up to this point, and they were well up on the Roman Wall just below the summit of Mt. Baker. All of a sudden the whole mountainside cut loose and started to slide down the south face. This avalanche caught all the members of the party, and they began to rapidly descend down the mountain. Some who were on the sides of the avalanche were able to escape; however, many were right in the middle. Some rode out the avalanche and stayed on top of the snow, but a number disappeared within the snow. The area to search was vast. The avalanche had traveled down the mountain approximately half a mile.

The two, after settling down to a cup of coffee at Bill's dining room table, continued to tell the story. Their party had spent from approximately noon until the end of the day searching. These two were selected to travel down the mountain and go for help. They started searching immediately after the slide but found that the whole mountainside at that point was about to slide again. They waited about an hour to an hour and a half before they ventured out and started their search. When darkness set in, the whole group was to return to Kulshan Cabin and spend the night as they had the previous night.

Bill suggested that they return up the mountain and meet up with their group. He would start organizing a rescue party. The first thing that Bill had to do, with much regret, was to make two telephone calls, the first to the Whatcom County Sheriff's Department and secondly to the president of the college to make them aware of the accident.

He got on the rural telephone system and called the Maple Falls operator. He gave her instructions to place a call to the Sheriff's Department and next to the president of the college. Within a few minutes she called back with the Sheriff's Department on the line and he informed them of the accident and then requested their assistance. Next call came back from the college and with many regrets he had to inform them of the loss of some of their students. Bill knew that by the time these two conversations were completed, with the Maple Falls operator listening in, everyone in the town of Glacier would know of the incident. In fact, people were running from one house to the other and into the watering holes explaining and glorifying the accident on Baker.

In the meantime, Bill was thinking of how to put a large group of men together to head up the mountain. One of his first thoughts was to call the CCC Camp and request the assistance of foreman Don Blackman. Instantly the camp responded that they would provide 6 to 8 well-equipped mountain men within two hours, and they would

report to the Glacier Ranger Station. He then put a call in to all of his off-duty rangers requesting that they also report in two hours. He placed a call to the Austin Pass Ranger Station and asked that the stretchers and bamboo poles that were stored there be brought down to Glacier. He asked that the equipment from the Silver Fir Ranger Station be brought down also.

Stu, Little Joe, and the Brown brothers were talking over the situation in the main street of Glacier. They all thought that they should volunteer up at the Ranger Station and go up on the mountain to give a hand. None of them had any previous experience on a high mountain or with glacier travel. Stu knew that if he was going up on that bloody mountain, he needed extremely warm boots and clothing.

The group walked from Glacier up to the Ranger Station and let the word be known that they were willing to provide help for the search, and they could be ready in an hour. Bill, in talking to the group, said yes, he needed additional help, and he would be happy to hire these young men. He also insisted that they go home and get all the warm clothing that they could find.

At the designated time, the group met at the Ranger Station with many others. There was Bill Parke, with three other Rangers, six CCC Boys, and this group of young men from Glacier. Each of them was loaded with a heavy pack and sleeping bags, all provided by the Forest Service. This was the initial group that took off in the darkness with flash lights heading up the Mt. Baker Trail, the same trail that was used for the marathon races. A second group, mainly support, were planning to leave at eight

**KULSHAN CABIN USED AS BASE OPERATION FOR
THE MT. BAKER AVALANCHE**

Kulshan Cabin was used for years as the base camp for parties climbing
Mt. Baker. The cabin was jointly constructed by Western Washington College
and the Mt. Baker Club. After years of hard use and long winters, the Forest
Service finally removed the cabin. (J. Hanson)

Panorama of searching Party Crossing Snow Bridge On Coleman Gl

10:00 A.M.   7/23/39

10:00 A.M.   7/23/39

**LEADING THE RESCUE PARTY ACROSS COLEMAN GLACIER
AND FINDING A ROUTE AROUND CREVASSES**
**By the time of the avalanche, the mountain glacier fields were cracking badly
and route finding was a challenge. (William Parke Report, Mt. Baker National
Forest Ranger-Western Washington University Archives, Bellingham, WA)**

o'clock in the morning along with a string of pack horses loaded to the hilt.

At this point, each of the 17 and 18 year-old young men were starting to grow nervous thinking about this adventure. None of them had ever been up on a high mountain or searched for lost climbers. What if they found one of the deceased climbers? Stu thought that over the years, he had been protected by his mother. He had ventured out a few times with his friends for a good

adventure, but this was different; yet his mother had quickly agreed for him to go.

The rescue party arrived at Kulshan Cabin at 3 AM the following day. The following morning everyone in the cabin was up at 5 AM preparing to head up the mountain. Stu and the boys were placed in various teams and were taught how to rope up for glacier travel. The radio equipment which was provided by the Forest Service was reasonably

Labels within image:
SUMMIT MT. BAKER ELEV. 10.750
ROMAN WALL
Start of avalanche
Route of Climbers
PATH OF AVALANCHE
DEMING
½ Mile Slope Dist
Route of Searching Party
Miss Beers Rescued here in chimney
GLACIER
Ice Fall 100' high
Spot where Miss Tomes' Body was found
Note Avalanche Jumped Crevasse
Spot where Julius Dorn bluf's Body was found
Lower Limit of Avalanche
Panorama of Mt. Baker Avalanche 1939
NOON 7/23/39

TOTAL ACCIDENT SCENE AS VIEWED FROM THE SADDLE
This very detailed picture shows all of the facts and location of the accident.
(William Parke Report, Mt. Baker National Forest Ranger-Western
Washington University Archives, Bellingham, WA)

effective on the glacier but could not reach back to the Ranger Station in Glacier. The radio messages that were to be directed back to the Ranger Station were answered up on Church Mountain Fire Lookout, and then the fire watchman relayed the message by telephone back down to the Ranger Station.

The hike up Coleman Glacier was uneventful except for zigzagging in and around large crevasse fields. The party crossed through the saddle and came upon the scene of the accident directly ahead of them. Stu had studied the resolves of avalanches on Church Mountain from the front porch of Graham's. Many started near the top and ran down avalanche chutes all the way into the timber. This slide had occurred up on the Roman Wall and extended most of the distance down the length of Deming Glacier. He couldn't believe the size and the distance it

Searchers (left to right)
Ray Bright, Chet, Ullin,
Bill Parke, Don Blackman,
looking over lower portion of
slide from rocky ledge.

10:00 A.M. 2/24/39

**DISTRICT RANGER BILL PARKE LOOKING OVER
AREA TO BE SEARCHED**
**The planning of the search effort was a major task, and the importance of
doing it in a safe manner was obviously discussed. (William Parke Report,
Mt. Baker National Forest Ranger-Western Washington University Archives,
Bellingham, WA)**

traveled.

After the initial avalanche, three of the party, all from the Western group began their search and worked in extremely dangerous conditions. After hours of brutal searching they realized that there would be no more living victims to be found and retreated out of the danger.

As the rescue teams were given instructions to begin the search, an added team of a professor and three other students arrived from Western and joined in the operation. Stu's team was given an area to search and headed that direction. The leader was extremely careful crossing large crevasses in the face of the glacier.

The crevasses were large enough to hold a fully-loaded logging truck. As they approached an ice fall area, they could see something lying at the base of one of these ice cliffs. Coming up on the area, they could see that this was one of the victims. The person had fallen over a hundred foot ice cliff.

As they approached the body, Stuart who was in the back of the rope team, had a sudden feeling that he should untie himself and get the hell out of there. What was he doing here?

Reaching the body, they determined that it was, in fact, a missing woman mountain climber from the party. The leader of the group radioed to Bill to tell him of their discovery and requested that a body bag and toboggan be brought forward. As the group busied themselves gathering all of the climbing equipment nearby, Stu realized that there was a hushed silence within the group.

100

Dornblut's body
Prepared for transit

Hole where Dornblut's
Body was found

**LOCATION OF AVALANACHE VICTIM AFTER FALLING
OVER ONE HUNDRED FOOT ICE CLIFF**
The two located victims were partially buried and easily dug out. (William
Parke Report, Mt. Baker National Forest Ranger-Western Washington
University Archives, Bellingham, WA)

Part of Rescue Party pulling Body of Julius Dorn blot down West Side of MT Baker
3.00 P.M   7/23/39

**BODY OF ONE OF THE AVALANCHE VICTIMS BEING
TAKEN DOWN COLEMAN GLACIER**
**(William Parke Report, Mt. Baker National Forest Ranger-Western
Washington University Archives, Bellingham, WA)**

Within half an hour, a two-man party arrived with the body bag and the men on the site placed the young woman in the body bag. It wasn't an easy task as the body was frozen. Stuart could hardly handle the situation, but he did not allow himself to act like anything other than a man.

This group spent the rest of the morning searching and probing the snow in search of other victims. By the middle of the afternoon, the heat of the day was making the area extremely unsafe. Large blocks of ice were cracking and breaking off in the area of the ice fall. The group, including Stu, pulled back up on the mountain and got up on a rocky ridge. Stu then realized that he hadn't had anything to eat since morning and as his body started to shake, he wondered if it was due to the lack of food or what he had been part of.

As the group proceeded with the body down the dangerous Coleman Glacier, they came across a group of CCC men who were taking the body of one of the other victims, a man, down the mountain. The bodies of these two were being taken down the mountain and back to Glacier. Stu thought about this young girl and wondered about her life, what she might've been. What a terrible way to treat a girl dragging her down the mountain side, but there was really no other way. They continued down to the edge of the glacier, and the bodies were placed on two litters, then carried down to Kulshan Cabin. It became very apparent that everyone in the initial rescue party was now at a point of exhaustion.

They found the area at the cabin to be a sea of activity. There were many support people, horse pack trains with all kinds of supplies, and newspaper reporters.

**BRASS PLAQUE WITH THE NAMES OF THE
MT. BAKER AVALANCHE VICTIMS**
**Plaque is mounted on the face of a stone monument at Western Washington
University. (M. Impero)**

As Stu attempted to walk around the edge of the group of people, he walked into Boog, the daughter of Charlie Bourn of Glacier. She was as shocked to see him as he was to see her. She told him the following story. "My father came and got me and said that I needed to take a reporter from the Seattle PI up to the accident base camp. I looked at him in a state of disbelief because I am only 13 years old. Dad said that I was the only one of his packers left that could take this fellow up the mountain, so I finally agreed that I would do it. I told him that I had never been up this trail before and I wasn't sure I knew where it was.

"He told me that I needed to just head up Mt. Baker Trail and follow the horse shit. Well, here I am and all I want to do is get the hell out of here."

The support ranger came up to Boog and Stu and said, "I've got a project for you two, and I would appreciate it if you would get along with it right now. Boog, what I want you to do is go back to Glacier with your horse and a pack horse. On the pack horse, we will put the body of the fellow over there and Stu, I'd like you to go along in case she has any kind of problem."

Bill had advised me that he wanted all of the young men of Glacier, when they returned back to camp, to head back down to Glacier. As the others had not yet returned, Stu was appointed to go down with Boog. The search had become a body removal operation only.

With that, the ranger led one of the Bourn horses over to the location of one of the bodies, and some of the men began to load the body on the horse, cowboy movie style. Stu stood there in disbelief. All he could think about was those early cowboy movies where the body was tied across the saddle and transported. Boog said nothing but Stu could see that her face was getting very white. As they prepared to leave, the reporter came over to Boog, took her picture on her horse and told her that she was the best guide he ever had. He said that he wasn't going any further up the mountain and that he could get all the information that he wanted right here.

As the time approached to head back down the mountain, one of the cooks from the camp came forward and gave them both a prepared lunch. He told

them that we would need this on the way back. The radio message had gone out that they were coming down with the first body, so everyone in Glacier was prepared.

Boog went down the trail first, riding her horse, with the second horse loaded with the body. Behind her Stu followed and couldn't help but think about the young man that was in that bag. His life was over. They stopped a few times for water, allowing the horses to drink, and themselves some lunch. After a three and a half hour trip, they came into Glacier dead tired. There were few words spoken.

They stopped at the Glacier Ranger Station where an ambulance was standing by and, with the help of the personnel at the station, the body was placed in the ambulance. With their orders complete, they continued a quarter mile down to the Bourn Stable. They unloaded the horses and Boog turned to Stu and said, "Well Stuart, I hope you can sleep tonight for I know that I'm not going to. If I had to share this event with someone, I'm glad it was you."

Stu turned slowly toward her and answered, "Likewise."

Stu went into town and went directly to find his mother. She came forward, gave him a big hug and could see tears in his young eyes. She spoke softly, "How are you Stu?"

He looked at her seriously and said, "Not worth a shit, and now I'm going to go home and go to bed."

The searching continued for a total of six days with only those two bodies recovered. The rest were left to the eternal grave of Mt. Baker. S.A. Weitman, the father of one of the victims, and his son arrived at base camp and continued to search with the others. In his grief he actually hampered the search operation. The organized searching was complete with every one called off the mountain. Weitman and his son continued to search over the next few years.

Stu thought of those two days up on the mountain many times and thought that someday he would revisit the site but not for a very long time.

❦

GLACIER MEDICAL

Stu was offered a new part-time job, but it took a great deal of persuasion with his mother. Earl had to assure her that it would be safe, that Stu would not be working with chainsaws or any other equipment, for that matter. She and Stu took a trip up into the mountains to see a crew of two men working at the job that he was expected to do. When she agreed that it should be safe, she made Stu promise, once again, to not run a chainsaw.

For Little Joe, the matter of having the proper clothing and footwear was easy. His father and two older brothers were loggers and he could very simply borrow them and look appropriate. In Stu's case it was a different matter. He had work clothing that was used at the Graham's Store but they certainly did not look like logging clothing. Earl found some old jeans, put suspenders on them, and found a striped work shirt. Stu then looked the part of a logger.

Little Joe had his driver's license at this time and they rode up to the worksite in his brother's 1938 Chevrolet pickup. Once they got up to the site, he

informed Stu that the pickup actually had very little brakes but it would be just fine.

The two Bottiger Brothers were selected by the Forest Service to log an area up the Hannegan Pass Road. This timber sale required the harvesting mainly of cedar trees, which would be made into roof shakes. The brothers would cut down trees and drag them to a common location with a Caterpillar, and then they would cut off blocks about 25 inches long with chainsaws. Little Joe and Stu would stand these blocks on end, cut off the bark area, and then split them into smaller blocks. They then were to load them in a flatbed truck.

The first day was going well, when all of a sudden Stu heard an awful scream. "God dammit, Leck, what the hell did you do?" Pamp yelled, holding his hand over his ear.

"Shit, Pamp, I didn't do a damn thing." Leck answered quickly.

"Get over here and take a look at my god damn ear," yelled Pamp with blood streaming down the side of his face.

Pamp had been working behind the Cat which Leck operated. After stopping, Pamp attempted to pull a cable choker from under a three-foot cedar log where it was hung up. The cable suddenly sprung loose, flew up, and hit him in the side of the head. After viewing the damage from a distance, Leck commented, "Well, you tore your ear halfway off and you're bleeding like a pig with his balls cut off."

Pamp wrapped a diesel-soaked work shirt around his head and ordered Leck, "Throw the god damn tools in the pickup and hop to it. Shut off the damn Cat. We better get to town and get me

NABOB INN
The Nabob Inn was located west of town and also provided lodging.
(F. Bottiger)

SAMSON RANCH RESTAURANT
The Samson Restaurant was made famous by its fried chicken dinners. This
building remains today and is used by Snowline as a clubhouse. (Whatcom
Museum, Bellingham, WA)

fixed. You better tell those two young fellows that we are quitting for the day and tell them to come on down to Glacier."

Having never been to a doctor in his life, Pamp went to find his mother to sew it up. He ordered Leck to go to his house, get a bottle of whiskey, and then come down to the ranch where his mother, Hazel Bottiger, had some level of nursing training. The two young men decided to follow the activity down to the farm house and see if they could be of any assistance.

Grandma Bottiger was babysitting Pamp's five-year-old son, Frankie, and when Frankie heard his father's truck, he went running to greet him. When the little boy saw all the blood, he started to cry and would not stop until Pamp shouted, "Damn it, Frankie, shut up."

"First, Mom, you are going to sew it back together, and, Leck, you are to hold it in place."

Pamp ordered, "Now pour about a third of the bottle of that whiskey on it and give me the rest to drink." It took about half an hour to get the ear attached with Pamp jerking around in pain. Leck worked to line up the ear and held it in the proper position as Grandma worked to sew it on.

After getting the stitches in with the bleeding stopped, Grandma Bottiger then wrapped his head with an old sheet. Pamp finally sat still and finished the bottle. "Well, it's getting late, let's call it a day. Maybe have a drink." Pamp saw the two young men standing in the background and said, "Well, boys, see you tomorrow."

As the two friends drove back up to Glacier, Stu made a comment to Little Joe, "That is one tough man."

Little Joe added, "The whole family is."

It had been three weeks since the ear accident and Pamp announced at work that he was going down to Ma's to take the stitches out. While Little Joe and Stu had already talked about this and thought that it would be quite entertaining to see the end of the show, they joined the party. They followed the Bottigers from Glacier down to the Bottiger's farm.

Removing the sheet, Pamp, Leck, Little Frankie, and Pamp's wife all agreed that it was healing nicely. Pamp added that it felt good but a little hot. He asked Frankie how it looked. After studying it front and back, Little Frankie answered, "Well, it's bright red, somewhat lopsided, and is sticking out off your head." Frankie then started to laugh.

"Get me a mirror for a look." said Pamp. "Well Frankie, I think you did a good job of describing it." After a little more thought, Pamp said angrily, "God dammit Leck, if you or anybody else tells me about having a lopsided ear I'll kick the shit out of them."

Grandma Bottiger added, "Henry, for god's sake stop swearing around your little son."

Little Joe and Stu waited for the day that some guy, after drinking all night at Graham's, would make a comment about the lopsided ear.

STRANGE ODOR

Doug Hamilton had opened Graham's at the normal 6:00 AM time and within fifteen minutes or so, five to six of the Boys would be in for their morning coffee. Doug knew all the

Boys well. This being January, about half of the Boys were unemployed loggers due to snow conditions and they were collecting their state "rock-in chair" payments.

Frank Bottiger, with son Leck, arrived first, then minutes later Jumbo Bill came in. An hour later Jake Steiner, and then Ray Bowtell walked in the door. This day Frank came in with a pair of nice new dress pants with suspenders. In Graham's there was a big pot belly stove set over in the corner. The Boys, after having too much to drink would leave their bar stool, go over and collapse into three huge old chairs around the stove and fall sleep.

Frank always sat at one end of the bar and by 2:00 PM he was beyond feeling pain of any kind. At one point all the boys moved to the other end of the bar, and commented about a bad odor at the opposite end of the bar. Doug investigated near where Frank was sitting and decided the bad odor had to be coming from Frank. "Frank," said Doug in a forceful voice, "you have soiled your pants; now get the hell out of here." Frank tried to do as ordered but fell off the stool. He got up, waddled out the door like a big fat old duck, not saying a word.

An hour and a half later, Frank came back in, having changed his clothes and took a stool drinking only coffee.

The next day Leck came in by

himself, talking about a suit that he had bought from Sears. His mother had measured him for it. The fit was perfect and it came with two pairs of pants, but he could only find one pair. He asked if anybody had seen or heard what may have happened to the other. "Couple of days ago, you came in with your old man and he had on a nice pair of dress pants. I think you better ask him if he remembers," stated one of the Boys.

The following day in came Leck with a sad look on his face, "You were right! I walked with him to the bar. He had my pants on and I never even noticed! I guess I should look at him more closely to see if he is wearing my damn clothes. Well, I started looking and out the back door were my new pants. I think he was trying to throw them away and they got hung up in a tree. I think I'll leave them be. After a few days of heavy rain they will be ok." After this rundown, Leck went back to drinking.

After an hour, one of the Boys came in looking for Leck. "Leck, I don't know whether you realize it or not, but your brand new Oldsmobile is sitting in the middle of the street running. Does this indicate that one can't shut off his brand-new Oldsmobile?"

Leck looked up at him slowly and said, "Well, I was so excited trying to find my pair of pants, I guess I just left her in the middle of the street. I'll go."

Year Number Five

JERRY'S EVENING WITH THE BANKERS

Stu was doing a very detailed job of cleaning the bar and restaurant section of Graham's, for this evening was a very special event. It was the monthly meeting of the Whatcom County Banking Association, and the group had reserved the whole Graham's Restaurant and Bar. Occasionally people reserved a table in Graham's but this was the first time that an association had reserved the whole facility. That was a big thing for Earl and could lead to something much greater, but he also was extremely nervous.

Earl was the maître d' for the evening but he was not sure what the duties of a maître d' actually were. Earl's wife and Stu were to wait tables, while Liz McKenzie, Stu's mother, was doing all the cooking. Word was that special guests were attending, with one being the woman president of the Bellingham National Bank. This bank was where Earl did all of his banking and he wanted to remain on good terms and show how professional his establishment was.

Of course, the early "Boys" came in at the normal time and were planning to make a day of it. Finally at 4:00 PM, Earl announced to the group that tonight was a private party and if they would move across the street to the Inn, he would pay for their drinks. Jerry Bourn arrived at the door at 5:00 and wanted in. Finally, with a sigh of relief, Earl got Jerry to go across the street.

"Stu, I want you to work in here tonight as a bus boy and waiter. Do you know what the hell you are to do with both of these duties?" asked Earl with a serious look.

"Mr. Graham, you have forgotten that I am from the great city of Seattle, and I am a young man of the city," replied Stu with a smile as he turned away. Stu had never been in any high class restaurant in his life.

It was time for the higher class patrons to arrive, and that they did with men in coats and ties, women in dresses and heels. Few late arriving "Boys" also showed, but Earl persuaded them with the free drink offer to go across the street.

Cocktails were done and dinner was being served. All was going well. Stu turned out to be a good waiter, liked by all the guests. Then the worst thing that could have possibly happened did. Jerry Bourn, who had been thrown out across the street, now wanted in Graham's. Earl and Stu blocked the front door and each time Jerry would try to get in, they would hold him back and return him to the street.

Jerry was dressed in his normal wool shirt and jeans held up by suspenders. The get-up had not been washed in months and neither had Jerry, with a full head of hair and a full beard.

Earl was standing in the doorway

109

**PEACEFUL, GENTLE JERRY BOURN IN HIS HOME–
THE CHARLIE ANDERSON CABIN**
**Jerry was the last of the mountain men in the Glacier District of the
Mt. Baker National Forest. Thirty-three years after his death, the legacy
of Jerry continues to grow. (J. Steiner)**

with his legs spread out and his arms out wide. Jerry got half way out in the middle of the highway and came running toward Earl. Earl expected an upper body collision but it didn't happen. Jerry dove low and went in between Earl's legs, shooting into the room on his belly. He was instantly up, and seeing a seat in a near booth, he sat down. Well, guess who Jerry was sitting beside? None other than the president of Earl's bank. Before long, the two were in a deep conversation with Jerry telling her all about Glacier and how the Graham's were great people.

Earl was beside himself not knowing what to do. He wanted to throw Jerry out, but that would cause a big scene and Jerry, usually in that kind of a situation, would piss his pants, which wouldn't be good. Earl, after a little while, went to the table to check and the woman president said everything was great, as she was having a conversation with Jerry.

"Earl, when is my dinner coming?" Jerry asked.

"I will check on it right now. That was a steak and baked potato, right Jerry?" replied Earl.

Jerry nodded his approval. When Earl came with the food Jerry was discussing gold with the banker. As the night went on, Jerry became the entertainment for the evening. All the people were gathered around him, listening to stories from growing up in Glacier, to gold mining, to stories of

110

being in WWII. During this time, Jerry had nothing more to drink.

In a few days, the banker called Earl to thank him for such a fine, fun, evening. She especially loved the live entertainment, this fellow named Jerry Bourn! She thought it was a creative idea to bring him in. She suggested that Earl have him in each weekend.

Earl assured her, "He will be here each weekend."

The banker added, "I recommend that you do something, however, about his body odor. When I got home I had to shower to get rid of that odor."

❦

FATHER AND SON TRIP TO TOWN

Stu was sitting outside Graham's on his favorite bench doing his schoolwork. On this bench, he could do his schoolwork and also catch up on all the activities that were going on in Glacier that day. He looked up and saw little Frankie Bottiger, coming from the direction of his house. Stu was well-liked by all the young kids in Glacier, as most of the other guys his age were all in a hurry to grow up, and they ignored the little kids. Frankie was just six or seven years old, and he obviously felt a strong companionship with Stu. He made a point of almost daily finding him and having some kind of a conversation.

As he approached with tears in his eyes, Frankie said, "Hi," in a very depressed state.

Stu realized very quickly that there

**LECK BOTTIGER ON THE LEFT WITH HIS BROTHER PAMP
NEXT ON THE RIGHT**
**Leck served in the Army and Pamp in the Navy in World War II with both
returning to Glacier and careers in the logging industry. (F. Bottiger)**

HORSESHOE SMOKE SHOP
The Horseshoe Cafe is in the same location on Holly Street for well over fifty years. (M. Impero)

was something wrong with the little guy and asked, "What's up Frankie, you seem troubled?"

"Well, my mother told me that maybe my dad and I would be going to jail. I know that they put old people like my dad in jail, but they don't put six-year-old kids in jail, do they Stu?"

Stu looked at him and answered, "No, I don't think so. They don't normally put six-year-old kids in jail, but what was this terrible crime that you and your dad committed?"

The story started three days earlier. Pamp announced his plan to go to Bellingham for bank business the next day and was expected to be gone most of the day. Ella, Pamp's wife, knew very well what happened each time Pamp had a business trip to Bellingham. He would arrive back after midnight in a dreadfully drunk state. "Pamp, Little Frankie needs some new shoes. Why don't you take him with you?" Ella asked.

What could Pamp say? "Why sure, Frankie and I will make a day of it, right Frank?" Pamp replied.

After a few stops on the way, they

were in town. The Bellingham National Bank was half a block from Pamp's chief watering hole in town—the Horseshoe Café on Holly Street. The banking business only took fifteen minutes and then it was off to the Café for an early lunch. Always, when he was in the bank building, Pamp would go to his safety deposit box, check out and review his immense stamp and coin collections. Like every other time, he found everything in order.

"Well, Frankie, what would you like for lunch a steak, hot dog, or a hamburger?" Pamp asked the six year old.

Having never been to town with his dad before Frankie shook his head.

"Ok, Frankie, you can't decide. Let's have sirloin steak with fries, ok?" asked Pamp.

Frankie only looked at him with a blank look.

Pamp continued, "Now, I'm running into the other room to get a drink and will be right back." Off he went to the bar.

Little Frankie sat eating his french fries. After an hour his dad returned.

"Why aren't you eating your steak? Jesus Christ, I'm spending good money on that slab of meat," Pamp demanded.

Little Frankie answered, "I don't know how to eat it. Do I pick it up in my hands and chew on it or what?"

Pamp raised his voice "Jesus Christ, didn't your mother teach you how to eat a steak?"

About this time, the cocktail waitress brought two more doubles for Pamp. He tried to encourage his son to stop crying and eat the damn meat. Two more doubles and a chocolate sundae followed, then two more doubles and apple pie with ice cream.

About 8:30 Pamp said, "Frankie, it's about time I get you home."

Before starting home, Pamp and Frankie both fell asleep in the front seat of Pamp's pickup. In the Rome straight away, Pamp pulled over and woke up Frankie and said, "I'm too sleepy to drive. You should take over."

Well, Frankie was only six years old, but had driven the farm tractor down on the farm. He looked up at his father with a look of "What?"

Frankie had driven the pickup down at the farm sitting on his dad's lap but this was entirely something different.

"Well, you sit on my lap and steer and I will run the throttle and brake, Frankie," Pamp ordered.

Frankie hopped on his dad's lap and they started home at ten miles per hour. Every so often the pickup would slow down to nothing and Frankie would have to wake up his dad. Somehow they made it into Bottiger's farm about two miles from the town of Glacier.

Pamp told Frankie that he was going to sleep at Ma's and told him to go home to their house. Frankie walked

the two miles home to Glacier on the side of the Mt. Baker Highway in the dark. As he walked into the house, his mother was in a state of disbelief. After getting Frankie settled in for the night, she went down to Grama's and beat the hell out of Pamp. Pamp had forgotten the shoes.

Stu sat there looking at Frankie in total disbelief. How possibly could a six-year-old boy possibly drive a car from Bellingham to Glacier in the dark and not be involved in an accident?

Finally Stu asked Frankie, "You drove that car basically all the way home?"

Frankie answered, "Well, I was doing the steering but dad was doing the gas and the brake, when he was awake." Stu just sat there and looked at Frankie in total disbelief.

Stu said, "Frankie, no police have come for you yet. There haven't been any reported accidents and there must not be any new dents in the pickup so, I guess I would forget the whole thing. Maybe, it's not a good idea for you to go to town with your dad for a while, you should probably wait until you're a little bit older. How are your mother and dad getting along now?"

Frankie answered slowly, "Well, dad hasn't been at the house the last three nights and mom said that he will never be allowed in again."

Stuart told his mother Frankie's whole story. They were both very concerned about him and his older sister's well-being. Liz instructed him to keep an eye on the house and the stories that were floating around town.

The town was routinely quiet at 9:30 on this regular Thursday night, except for the two watering holes, but there

PAMP AND ELLA BOTTIGER
(F. Bottiger)

was a sudden blast of yelling along with a mixture of profanity. All of a sudden porch lights all over town came on and people were out for a look. The noise came from Pamp Bottiger's home. Soon a group of neighbors headed down to Pamp's thinking there might be a medical problem or even a fire.

Little Joe came charging through the front door of the McKenzie's cabin. He said, "I think old Pamp is as drunk as a skunk, and his wife has locked herself in the bathroom!"

Stu, his mother, and Little Joe all hurried in the direction of the Bottiger house. When they got there they realized that the whole population of Glacier was out in the street in front of the house. Pamp was screaming like hell at Ella to let him in.

"I think I heard that it started three weeks ago when Pamp wore his cork boots into the living room with the new white rug," stated little Joe.

Pamp came back outside, yelling profanity at the gathered group.

He ran to his pickup, got out a Homelite chain saw, started it up, and walked back towards the home. His two little kids that were inside came running out.

The saw powered up to full power and cutting took place. In less than a minute, the saw was shut off, and Pamp returned to the front door throwing the saw into the yard.

"I'm coming in, bitch!" yelled Pamp.

Pamp had cut a second doorway into the bathroom wall, cutting through water pipes and electrical wiring.

Little Joe looked at Stu and replied, "Typical night here in Glacier."

❦

NELSON'S RACE CAR

Stu sat at a table near the post office area in Graham's doing school work. A very loud rumbling came from across the creeks in the east section of Glacier. All of a sudden, the Boys in attendance began to talk excitedly. Stu moved closer to get the story. "Well Kid, Bud Nelson is back in town and he must be going to take the old "39" for a test burn," Earl reported. "His race car goes like a bat out of hell. He is an expert with gas motors. Rumor had it, that the Hauser people in Indianapolis wanted to hire him to work on their race cars. He declined thinking that Glacier had a better future for him."

Stu noticed that all the Boys were busy doing something at the bar. He

114

BUD NELSON WITH THE #39–GLACIER'S ONLY RACE CAR
Bud raced #39 on various tracks in Canada and Washington State. One can only imagine that there was no safety equipment in this race car. The one thing that is noted is that there is no rollover bar. (R. Nelson)

determined that they were forming some kind of betting pool. They were betting on Nelson's time to go down the highway to the Warnick Bridge, turn at Steiner's, and then take the old road back to town. Earl was keeping the bets. The man closest to the actual time would win. Each man made a five dollar bet.

Jake said, "He is about ready to run her out into the brush again. God help him if he rolls her again. I'm going with seven minutes and forty-five seconds."

Earl added that his best time was seven minutes and twenty seconds. With the bets all in the pot, the boys stood by with drink in hand.

Now the Boys, Earl, and Stu moved to the front boardwalk and noted that across the street all the dogs in town, big and small, were lined up for

the chase. The dogs would all give up within a block or two and make preparation for the return chase. With the motor warmed up, all the mothers had plenty of time to get their little kids inside.

After the warm-up period, Bud came like a bat out of hell. He went through town like a flash and then the sound died down. The Bottiger dogs, down on the farm, gave chase. The whole distance the scream of the motor could be heard and as the sound grew louder, he was returning.

Earl had a job for Stu. "I want you to go out and look over the front windows facing the highway and see if there is any broken glass. Make it quick! Come in here before he gets back to town."

In doing so, Stu took note that all the Boys went back inside. With Bud almost to town, all the dogs took off

WARNICK LUMBER MILL
The Warnick Lumber Mill was the largest lumber mill in the area and was
located west of town. In the mid-1940s, it was destroyed by fire. (J. Steiner)

WARNICK MILL LOGGING CAMP
(J. Steiner)

running to meet him. As he flew by like a shot, they all turned and took chase. Flying past Graham's, Earl stopped the watch as Bud had to make a sharp left turn. As he turned, a wall of rocks coming off the gravel street shot up toward the front of the store.

Earl noted that Jumbo Bill was the winner. Stu went out to see if any windows had been broken this time. Stu returned and stated, "Well, Earl, I think he got two or maybe three panels."

Earl went behind the bar, did a little paper work, and returned giving him a paper. "Stu, will you take this up to Bud's place and give it to him? I have extra glass cut to size for this type of problem."

Stu walked to Bud's house. He read the bill:

> To: Bud Nelson, Glacier - Charge for breaking three windows @ $5 each. You had one of your best runs ever, seven minutes and ten seconds. Earl

❧

DAISY, THE COW

Stu again sat on the bench at Graham's. This time settled in next to him was a new girl in town named Sue Miller. Sue was his first girlfriend. She was there living with grandparents and was planning to go to Mt. Baker High School in the fall.

All of a sudden, Stu could see little Frankie coming up the street. When he got close, Frankie asked Stu, "Stu, will you go to the farm and see if we can find my old Daisy?"

"Yes, we will go down this afternoon and take a look for your cow," answered Stu.

Sue jumped into the conversation and added, "I'd like to go, too. "

Stu advised little Frankie to meet them at three o'clock at Graham's and they all would go down.

As soon as Frankie was out of hearing distance, Sue asked Stuart, "What's the story on the cow?"

Stu looked at her and began to tell the story. "Well, as you know, the Bottiger's have a herd of cattle down at the farm and Frankie has been very attached to one old cow which he named Daisy. He would sneak down to the farm and before long he was riding on her back. Within a few weeks he'd come riding the cow to Glacier sitting high and proud on the cow's back. Frankie would ride into the Glacier area and we'd hear a clump, clump, clump sound. He would come into town, get off the cow, but then have a major problem getting back on. Somebody would have to help. Sometimes when he brought the cow to Glacier, he just turned her loose, and she went to everybody's flower and vegetable gardens. Everyone gave Frankie and his dad, Pamp, hell over it.

"Well, one day little Frankie was down at the farm riding Daisy and he fell off. He walked all the way to Glacier, crying and holding his arm. When he arrived home, he reported the accident to his father.

"Now, Pamp did not believe in doctors and all treatment was by either him or his mother. He ordered Frankie to release the arm but in doing so Frankie let out a scream as his arm flopped at a right angle.

"Pamp responded, 'I can fix it—you

YOUNG FRANK BOTTIGER'S PET COW
(F. Bottiger)

sit here and lay it flat. Now, stop that damn crying, you're acting like a baby!'

"Pamp found some old newspaper and electrical tape. Carefully he wrapped the arm with newspaper; then the electrical tape was wrapped around it. The job was finished by making a sling out of an old sheet.

"Okay, all done Frankie. It will be fine in three weeks. We will check it out," Pamp said.

"For weeks, the little guy hung around the house in pain. On the appointed day, all was ready for the inspection. First, Frankie was told to set his arm down on the table and lay it flat. Next, Pamp slowly removed the tape and newspaper. He told Frankie to move his arm off the table. It flopped as before with little Frankie letting out a blood curdling scream. After getting the arm back up on the table, Pamp said, 'Jesus Holy Christ, I think this arm is broken! We should take him to the doctor now.'

"From this point forward, Frankie was told he could no longer ride the cow and he was not allowed to go down to the farm by himself. After a few months, Frankie decided it was time to check out the cow. He waited until both his mother and dad were gone, then he walked down to the farm. He looked for two hours but couldn't find Daisy.

"A few days later, he begged his father to take him down so he could look. Pamp reluctantly agreed. After an hour of searching, Pamp said, 'There she is.'

"Frankie replied, 'No, that's not her.'

"Sometimes Frankie, wild animals, like a cougar or bear get a cow. That cow is no place to be found,' said Pamp."

Stu looked at Sue and said, "That brings you up-to-date with the story of Frankie's cow. He still goes down every chance he gets and searches for her. He realizes that if a cougar or bear got her he would find the horns of the cow.

Pretty smart little kid."

Later that day, the three of them went down for the cow search and again were unsuccessful, however the little guy talked about going down again the next day to continue the search.

One afternoon, Stu was in the back of Graham's store stocking shelves, when in came Pamp. He went directly over to Stu. Stu was concerned that he was going to catch hell. Pamp began, "Stu, I know that you are trying to help Frankie find the cow, and I appreciate you're helping him. You are an idol to my six-year-old son and I'm thankful for that. I am going to tell you of the whereabouts of that cow. When you drive by the Kendall store, the storefront reads: MEAT LOCKERS AVAILABLE."

Pamp continued, "Does that answer your question? Why don't you take Frankie down one day and see if he can pick out another cow but let's not encourage the riding."

Pamp turned to walk away and then turned back. He handed Stu a beautiful jackknife, then said, "This belonged to my grandfather. I'd like you to have it."

As Pamp walked away, Stu said to him, "Thanks a great deal, Pamp."

After Pamp walked away, Stu thought to himself, "That's the nicest thing I've ever heard him say to anybody other than to his wife and kids. I guess he can be a pretty nice fellow after all."

<hr/>

FRANK'S DEATH

Pamp came into Graham's store at his normal time. In Graham's, all of the Boys had their predetermined stools, and it was understood that when the Boys came into the bar, anyone that was on these stools were to move.

Pamp came in and ordered his usual drink and announced to the crowd that was present, "Well, Frank cashed her in last night. Oh, I guess I should say my father cashed it in last night. Got a call from Leck at 1:30 in the morning, which really pissed me off." With that he continued to drain his drink. All the people in Graham's sat there in a state of shock waiting for additional information. Frank had been a fixture in Glacier as long as anyone could remember. There were only two or three other people that had lived in Glacier longer.

Finally Earl said, "Well, Pamp you got a telephone call. Tell us a little more than that. Where did this happen, where is he, and when will he be getting back to town? What's the plan? "

Jumbo Bill added, "Pamp, where are Leck and Frank?" By this time Stuart and his mother were also in the bar and people were coming in off the street to hear the story.

Pamp began, "Leck has gotten in the habit of getting a new Oldsmobile each year. It's kind of hard to believe looking at Leck's one-year-old car and realize that it is not 10 years old. Now this year, Leck took Frank and headed east. He dropped the old man off at relatives in Wyoming and then continued to Detroit to get the new Olds."

"On his return trip, after picking up the old man, he continued his trip west. Well, last night at about 2 AM, I got a telephone call and I answered it, 'Who the hell is this, this better be good, god dammit.' Leck told me the story of heading home with Frank. He stopped in a town in Wyoming to pick up some beer and wine. Leaving Frank in the front seat sleeping, Leck spent a couple of hours in the bar. Returning to the car he attempted to wake up Frank but to no avail. Now, Leck wasn't much into checking if a person was alive or dead, but after a few minutes he decided the old man had died.

"Well, that's it—the old man cashed her in last night. They were someplace in Wyoming. Oh hell, not sure where they were."

Pamp continued, "What do I do with him?" Leck asked in his soft manner.

"Are you sure he's dead or has he just passed out?" Pamp asked. "I assume you can tell the difference. Well, I guess you better drive him home and then we will decide what to do with him. You bought air conditioning in the new car. If he starts to stink, turn it on and open the windows. Don't wake me again! I got to go to work tomorrow."

The phone went dead and Leck started the drive. When he ran out of wine, he would stop and get a refill.

Leck's last stop to buy wine before arriving back in Glacier was at the Kendall Store, eight miles down the road from Glacier. He realized that once he and Frank arrived in Glacier there would be many people viewing the body and there would be much discussion in the middle of the street.

As he walked into the store, Leck saw an old friend, Corky Smith, and started a conversation with him. The discussion got to the topic of Leck and Frank's trip. Leck told him of the new small whiskey bottles that were being served on airplanes. Leck was so intrigued with the small bottles that he bought two or three cases of them and had three or four bottles in his pocket.

He offered one to Corky and Corky said, "Well, let's have your dad come in and have a shot, too."

Leck said Frank was out in the car and he was quite stoved up. Corky then said that he would go out and help Frank get out of the car.

Finally Leck admitted, "Well, Frank is actually quite stiff. Oh hell, he's dead and I'm just driving back home."

Everyone's mouth dropped wide open and with that Leck gathered up his wine and headed home.

Leck and Frank arrived in Glacier on a Friday. The whole town had been waiting for their arrival and as he stopped, the whole town gathered around the car. Against the passenger side of the car, Frank appeared to be sound asleep. Pamp told Leck that he was really happy that the next day was Saturday because he could deal with the old man and not even miss a day of work.

Later in Graham's, Jumbo Bill had his first jumbo of the day. Jumbo said to Earl, "Well, one thing about it, Pamp should not have to spend any money on embalming costs because Frank has been pickled for years from alcohol. Ten years from now, I would assume he'd look exactly the same."

The following morning, Pamp walked down to the shack that Frank and Leck lived in. After getting Leck up, Pamp said, "Well, let's bury the old bastard today. I'll have Jumbo Bill and Peg Leg Mayheau dig a hole at the graveyard. I've gotten some 2 by 12 planks at the shop and you and I will build a box."

That afternoon with the whole town present, Frank was laid to rest in the Glacier Cemetery in the custom-made coffin created with painstaking care. Most of the old Boys were present.

Stu and his mother also attended the service at the cemetery. Pamp had found a minister of some sort. Stu and his mother were both shocked at this method of burial but everyone present felt that this was typical of the Bottigers.

After a few months, Pamp went to Bellingham on bank business. Afterwards, he purchased a headstone for Frank, then to the Horseshoe for lunch.

The headstone arrived in Glacier by freight truck in the middle of a winter snowstorm, so it was put into storage in Graham's storage room and Stu covered it up with empty beer bottles. Six to eight years later, someone finally questioned Pamp about why Frank didn't have a headstone. Then he remembered it. The next day, he and Leck went up and placed it on the ground, not knowing for sure if they got it in the right spot.

Year Number Six

HAZEL BOTTIGER'S DEATH

The whole town of Glacier was in a state of mourning. The day before, the beloved Hazel Bottiger had passed away in a Bellingham hospital of old age. Her funeral was to be held the following day in Glacier. Stu sat in the back of Graham's reading the obituary in the newspaper. This happened to be the first obituary he had ever read. Hazel had helped Stu many times with his homework. She had been a very good teacher. Grandma Bottiger had been loved by everyone in the area.

In her early life Hazel had been a teacher and had studied nursing. She taught for many years at the Glacier School. Following consolidation with the Maple Falls School she went on to serve on the school board. She was involved in all the activities of Glacier from helping with charitable work to the war effort. Her beloved Frank went from a handsome husband to a crotchety old man, but she maintained her dignity and respect.

After her death, Pamp and Leck put on one of the grandest funerals the town of Glacier had ever seen. The casket was made of solid wood, held together with silver hardware. This coffin was considerably different from what was used to put Frank in his final resting place. Hazel was buried beside Frank in the Glacier Cemetery and the service was held in the Glacier City Hall, with a procession afterwards to the cemetery.

The two Bottiger brothers were dressed in immaculate black suits just for the occasion, and Janet, their sister, was also dressed in a new black suit dress. Everyone east of Maple Falls was present. Following the service at City Hall, the procession moved to the cemetery. After the graveside service, the procession returned to Glacier. Most of the folks returned to their homes; however, the Boys returned to Graham's all dressed up.

Four days later, a group of Canadian tourists stopped at the Glacier Ranger Station to get directions to what they had been told was a beautiful cemetery in the area. The ranger gave them directions to the Glacier Cemetery. The group found the cemetery, but also found a casket sitting high and dry. They returned to the ranger station and told him of their discovery.

That evening, the ranger walked down to Pamp's and said there was an issue at the cemetery. Pamp looked sharply into the ranger's eyes, and said "Oh, hell, I forgot to get her in the ground!"

❧

CODE OF GLACIER

Stu was anxious to get home to Glacier. His mother and he had gone to Seattle to visit relatives. After two weeks they were both ready to return. As they came into the town, everything looked exactly the same as when they had left. As they approached the cabin,

123

LOCATION WHERE JOHNSTONE'S CAR WAS FOUND IN THE NOOKSACK RIVER
(Jack Carver-Whatcom Museum, Bellingham, WA)

Earl Graham came out from the back of the store and asked them to come on in because there was something he wanted to tell them.

As his story began to unfold, it almost became more unbelievable. Earl said, "The events of the situation started the night that the two of you left to go to Seattle. Now that was Saturday night and everybody was in town having a good time. One of the boys that was here that night was Howard Johnstone. You will know who he is; he's been around here in the bar and is a buddy of Bud Nelson. Late in the evening an argument developed between him and one of the Boys. The argument got more heated and they each left separately.

"Following this argument, the rest of the Boys called her a night. Around 3 AM, I was awakened from a dead sleep by the sound of a bulldozer running. Now you know that right behind Graham's there's been a new logging road being constructed up there.

Well, I could not believe there was a bulldozer operating at that time of night and so I went out on the boardwalk to investigate. There I met up with three or four people all there with the same question. 'Well,' we all said, 'what the hell?' And went home to bed.

"On Monday morning, family members of Howard Johnstone's from Bellingham called to Glacier concerned because he hadn't returned. The first thought was that he had gone someplace with his Glacier friends, and being unemployed at the time, would return soon. On Wednesday morning, with still no word of his location, friends from Glacier and Bellingham started the search. The first thing they did was to drive down the highway from Glacier toward Bellingham attempting to find where he may have run off the road.

"Late Wednesday morning, Howard's car was located in the Nooksack River just downstream from Boulder Creek. The car had gone off a 30 foot cliff into

124

the river and was sitting on all four wheels in approximately one foot of water.

"The County Sheriff Deputy was called to the scene and the car had been drug out of the river by Billy Goat Wreckers. There was no sign of Johnstone around his car, and the County Sheriff came up to Glacier to investigate. At this point, the thought was that he drank too much, drove off the road over the short cliff, and got washed away by the river. Two strange things were found in all this. First the key was shut off in the car and, second, the water was only a foot or so deep.

"The deputy talked to many people concerning the events of Saturday night. No one had any information concerning one of the Boys and him having a heated argument. No one came forward with any information about the bulldozer running in the middle of the night. The deputy spent the bulk of the day in the Glacier area, and a search was initiated in the river from the car site down.

"More than a dozen searchers followed the river bank for more than three hours looking in the river and along the brush. They looked into the log jams and deep pools. Johnstone had a lifelong, faithful dog and it was brought up to help in the search. The search for the body or an injured Johnstone was discontinued after three days.

"The following weekend an airplane, piloted by Johnstone's brother-in-law, was flying up and down the river trying to see any signs of a body. The weather was relatively good and they made many trips. On their last pass they were just downstream from Maple Falls, making a very sharp turn, when the plane plunged to the earth. The brother-in-law and his passenger were both killed instantly. Within a short period of time, all searching for Johnstone was discontinued and the case was closed.

"No one spoke to law enforcement about the sound of the bulldozer the night that he disappeared. Who may have operated the bulldozer was not discussed either. Now I recommend for your well-being you both forget about what I have told you and do not discuss it around town here at all. I just thought you needed to know that old Howard Johnstone's not around anymore."

Earl went on, "You two are familiar with Six-Pack Ernie. As you know, Ernie is a great talker who loves to visit with anyone that will listen. He spends the bulk of every day in that logging truck with no one to talk to. Ernie became very fascinated with the Johnstone situation and every time anyone would listen, he would bring the subject up and go into great detail.

"Two nights ago, Ernie and his wife were getting ready for bed. All of a sudden, they heard a loud rifle shot. When he investigated, Ernie found that a bullet had gone through the front of the house all the way out through the back. At that point, he made it known that his interest in the Johnstone situation was no more."

Earl finished, "Remember the old saying, law enforcement stops at the Warnick Bridge."

MINING EDUCATION

Liz McKenzie was sitting in the back corner table of Graham's Restaurant enjoying her last cup of coffee for the day. She and Stuart had been living in Glacier for over five years and she was thinking about how well Stuart was doing. She had brought him here so that he would have male figures in his life to influence him and that had certainly happened. But, how was he really doing? That was the question. She thought about how he was doing in school, and he seemed to be doing very well. The school system at Mt. Baker High School certainly did not meet the criteria of the Seattle schools but he was doing very well compared to the other students. However, there were very few students and some of them could absolutely care less about school.

Stu had made a lot of friends with all the local boys his age and was friendly with all of the local girls. He now had developed a love of history and when he had no homework to do, he would research the local history in Glacier.

Liz realized that while Stu had men to influence his life, she was concerned that he was becoming almost one of them. She had not heard him use much profanity, at least around her, or use tobacco around her. He still worked steadily for Earl Graham at the store, and he was also talking about going into the Army following graduation from high school. He also had the vision of going to college to study history.

Liz had written to her sister in Seattle many times describing who Stu was becoming. Her sister constantly reminded her that was what she wanted. In the very beginning, most of the old-timers would not give him the time of day and he was known as "City Slicker Kid."

As time went on his name was shortened to "The Kid." Now Stu could have a running conversation with any of the old Boys anytime he wanted. Old Frank Bottiger would sit out in front of the store on the bench and spend hours talking to him about a variety of topics. When they didn't have a topic to talk about, old Frank would ask him to name the state capitals. Frank was very good at the state capitals; never missed one, but now his student never missed one either.

If Stu was ever in trouble, the Boys kept it to themselves but made him pay one way or the other. Sometimes they covered up stuff and didn't let his mother know.

Most of Stu's friends were good-hearted kids with loving parents. Many of them had planned a lifetime of working in logging camps in the national forest, with no plans for further education.

Before her sudden death, Hazel Bottiger went into Graham's to get her mail and upon seeing Liz, came over and joined her. Hazel had many years of teaching experience and had been on the school board at the Maple Falls School District. Liz asked Hazel, "Do you think that the children at the Mt. Baker High School are getting an adequate education?"

Hazel answered, "I think they're getting the best education that they can get in such a small school. The school provides good education in the classes that are provided, however it does not provide much variety. You obviously are concerned about Stuart's education. I can honestly say that it is not the quality of a Seattle school; however, he's getting an education in many other ways. That young man has exceptionally high quality standards and that was all inspired by you. I do believe that you did the right thing by moving up here. and I'm sure that if you asked him today he would have absolutely no regrets."

Hazel continued, "The men folk here in Glacier are a very hard-core group. They work extremely hard, drink way too much, and are ready to fight at the drop of a hat. These are the men that Stuart is being exposed to and the question is, 'What is he getting out of it?' The one thing that I will say about the men folk hanging around Glacier, including my late husband Frank and my two sons, is that they have tremendous respect for all the women and a love for any kid in the area." With that Hazel continued her trip home and Liz sat smiling, agreeing with everything that was said.

On a warm Saturday morning in July, the large pot belly stove in Graham's was to receive its summer cleaning. The stove was at the far end of the bar and had an area surrounding it that was filled with sand to prevent a fire. None of the "Boys" was on hand and Earl got Stu started on the project.

They were startled when a sober, cleaned up Jerry Bourn said, "Morning boys. How are you doing, Earl, and how is the Kid?"

Earl asked, "Jerry, I haven't seen you in a month or so, what you up to?"

"Oh," replied Jerry, "I've been back on Silesia Creek working my Red Lead Claim. I had a good month on the creek and came to square up with you, Earl."

Jerry always owed Earl for

something, but Earl never expected to get any payment. "You remember the time last year that I threw the big boulder through the front window with me attached and also the time I fell off the bar stool on the table and ruined it? Well, it's time to pay up." Jerry handed Earl a small glass tube filled with gold and added, "This should pay for those items and I should have a little on credit. How about a cup of your gut rot coffee? Hey, Kid, if you want some damn good coffee, come to my cabin." After an hour of conversation, Jerry left.

After Jerry's departure, Earl stood behind the bar staring at the tube of gold. About that quick, Stu was right beside him for a look. Earl got out a sheet of black paper, opened the tube, and poured the contents onto the paper. "Stu, this is the real thing. Old Jerry goes back on Silesia Creek and comes out with a different amount each trip. Nobody knows where he goes but he always comes out with gold. Now, look here. People think that gold in a natural state is round like perfect round balls. Well, it's not. Gold is found in all shapes and sizes, but mainly very small pieces like these. See these are all different shapes." Earl went to a drawer and found a magnifying glass. "Here, look at this piece. It's called wire gold. See the small wires that make it up?"

Earl began to tell the story of the Mt. Baker Gold Rush. "Three men from Sumas, Jack Post, Russ Lambert, and Luman Van Valkenburg discovered the now famous and rich Lone Jack claims. They had been camped at Twin Lakes. Jack Post had traveled south on the east side of Bear Mountain and discovered the three rich veins of gold-bearing ore. Hell, when those boys made that discovery, that area was an absolute wilderness. They discovered that gold in August of 1897. The road went no further than Loop's Corner, which was just east of Maple Falls. From that point on, it became a very crude trail and the trail forded the Nooksack River numerous times. Many big creeks, such as Glacier Creek, were crossed. With this discovery came a tremendous influx of people who created and settled the town of Glacier.

"There were thousands of mining claims in the Mt. Baker Mining District; however only two of them really proved to be rich and were operated for many years. The first one was the Lone Jack, which was discovered by the three boys from Sumas. The second was the Boundary Red which was situated almost in Canada on the backside of Red Mountain. Both of these mines and all of the others were accessible only in the summer time, however crews spent the whole winter working both mines.

"Old Charlie Bourn, yes the same Charlie that you know here in town, was the most famous of all the packers. The packers transported all the goods, construction equipment, and materials into the mines. Both of these mines were accessible only by mountain trails and these trails were not wide enough for any kind of wheeled traffic.

"Up the river, near the last bridge, was a small town called Shuksan. The highway camp is located there. This town was created because of the gold rush and it existed for about 8 to 10 years. At one point it had its own post office, numerous stores, and a livery stable.

"Jerry was exposed to all these early miners at a very young age. There was Charlie Anderson, Amos Zimmer, Bert Lowry, Jack Post, and many more. These old timers would meet here almost every afternoon. They sat around that potbellied stove and told tales of the gold that they found or were still searching for. Jerry would sit there for hours listening to the stories. At a young age, he and his brother, Tom, had a thorough knowledge of mining operations in the area. It's not surprising that Jerry, to this day, is very involved with mining. Everything Jerry tells me about gold in these mountains I believe."

After putting the gold in the back of a drawer, Earl continued, "I appreciate Jerry paying up his bill, but this converting gold to money is a real problem. Years ago you could walk into most businesses and they would exchange gold for regular money. Not today. Today, the law requires that it be sold to the federal mint in Seattle. Well, that is a true pain in the ass—this being such a small amount. Actually the place to sell real gold is to a Chinese man in Canada. I think I'll take this to Robert Averill, the jeweler in town. He is the guy who owns the Saginaw Mine up near Twin Lakes."

The two sat for a minute or two, then Stu said, "I can't believe that is the same Jerry that comes in here getting plastered and raising hell. Who is this guy?" Stu turned to Earl expecting an answer.

"Jerry, first off, is a very bright fellow, did real good in school, and should have gone to college," replied Earl. "His mother died when he was only five. Both Charlie and Jerry's mother had a great influence on him, both in different ways. His mother was an educated woman. She worked with Jerry on classroom learning at an early age. Jerry learned about horses and was most interested in the care and treatment of their injuries. Some feel that he could have become something in the medical field.

"People think there were two events in Jerry's life that made him what he is today. First was the death of his mother at his young age and secondly the divorce from his wife. Jerry married a woman by the name of Betty O'Brien. After the marriage, Jerry moved to her home town of Tacoma. Shortly after WW II broke out, Jerry joined the army. A short time later, Jerry received a 'Dear Jerry letter' and that was followed by divorce papers. Those two events impacted him a great deal. Well, we better get back to work."

For the next few weeks, Stu thought a great deal about Jerry Bourn. When Jerry was sober he was a most interesting man. Stu decided to pay Jerry a visit for some "damn good coffee." Stu's mother was planning a trip back to Seattle to visit. Stu was going to remain in Glacier so that he would not miss any school. His mother left on a Monday and Stu had decided that he would skip school and pay Jerry a visit. Not knowing if Jerry would be home, Stu decided to take a chance. Jerry had no electric power, no telephone, and his address was "General Delivery, Glacier, Washington." He picked up his mail about every three months.

Stu had decided that he would hop a ride on one of the logging trucks that passed through Glacier about every few minutes. He sat on the bench waiting until a truck came headed up the hill. The driver was Six-Pack Ernie. He stopped for his normal brew. Stu climbed into the truck and was told that he was going to Anderson Creek. He asked Ernie if he would let him off at Jerry's road. Ernie said, "Sure." He popped a top, and asked Stu if he wanted a cold one. It was 9:00 AM.

Stu climbed over oil cans, chains, and axes as he got out of the truck. He could hear Jerry's dogs barking wildly even before he got to the driveway. Ernie threw three beer cans in the bushes.

In full view of the cabin he could see five dogs sitting on the top of their dog houses barking like mad. Before Stu got to Jerry's driveway, he could hear the dogs going wild. Across the driveway was another dog guarding the entry. Stu stood in one spot, not knowing what to do next. He saw the door open a couple of inches and a rifle barrel pointed out. Jerry yelled, "Don't come any closer, I've got you covered. Who the hell are you and what the hell do you think you want?"

Stu answered, "Jerry, this is Stu, the City Slicker Kid from Glacier. Came up to have some damn good coffee."

Jerry responded, "Stay where you are till I get these god damn dogs under control." After yelling to shut the hell up, they all sat quietly on their dog houses and watched. The one guarding the driveway sat as Stu walked by. He didn't pet her.

When Stu got to the front door, he saw that almost all the exterior walls were covered with animal heads and hides. There were deer, bear, mountain goats, and hides without any fur left on them. All of a sudden, a human head shocked him. As he slowed for a

JERRY BOURN AT HOME AT THE FORMER
CHARLIE ANDERSON CABIN

This cabin was of very unique construction; all hand-hued old growth cedar trees. Charlie Anderson built this cabin with the help of a young boy named Jerry Bourn. The hand-split cedar planks of the roof had to be about eight to ten feet long. Charlie filed on four mineral claims and built the cabin on the one nearest to the river. The claims proved to be of no value, so after many years the Forest Service took action to have Charlie removed from the land. Upon Charlie's death, Jerry took over and moved in. A battle was waged between Jerry and the Forest Service that went on until Jerry's death. The Forest Service tried everything they could to have him removed but to no avail. Note: In this photo there are two horses and all of Jerry's dogs. In the lower left, a hood of an old Chevrolet which was used as a sled in winter. Also, in the insert, note the human skull. (Whatcom Museum, Bellingham, WA)

second look, Jerry said, "Oh you like my human head? Well that was my first wife."

As Stu entered the cabin, the smell of smoke was overwhelming. Everything was covered with a film of soot and dust but he could smell the coffee and the pot of stew that was cooking on the stove. In the corner was a wood stove and in the middle of the room was a small table with three chairs. Along the back wall was nothing but reading materials: newspapers, magazines, and books. There was also a ladder/stairs that led to the second floor sleeping room.

Jerry got Stu a cup of coffee. Stu took one look at it and asked for sugar. It was the blackest coffee that he had ever seen in his short life.

Jerry answered, "My coffee is so

**CHARLIE ANDERSON/JERRY BOURN CABIN
AT THE MOUTH OF SWAMP CREEK**
Note the winter supply of wood and steel cables used for the dog runs.
(G. Byeman)

good there's no need for sugar or cream."

In disbelief he looked closer. "Jerry," asked Stu, "Why are there egg shells in your coffee?"

"Oh, City Boy, it keeps the coffee from getting bitter," replied Jerry, "plus it keeps the coffee grounds in the bottom of the pot."

After studying the cabin a bit more Stu asked, "Did you build this here cabin?"

"No" Jerry began. "No, an old friend of mine did, well I actually did help. Charlie Anderson was his name and he discovered gold on this site, filed on four mineral claims, and built this here cabin. When I was about your age, my old man was doing a lot of packing in these mountains for miners. This is the Hannegan Pass Trail and in the summer

I'd go with him. We always stopped to visit Charlie.

"Now if Charlie needed help in building this cabin, my old man would say, 'Ok Jerry, you stay and help Charlie. I will pick you up on the way home.' I had no idea how long the old man was going to be gone so I would hang out and help Charlie. So, you see, in a way I did help build it.

"When I went into the War, Charlie got sick and moved down to Glacier. By the time I returned, Charlie had died. When I got home I was in trouble in no time with the law, so I moved up here to keep myself out of trouble, except it didn't work completely. Come and give me a hand putting some things in my refrigerator."

Stu looked around the cabin and not seeing anything that looked like a

THE JERRY BOURN CABIN IN THE MIDDLE OF A WINTER SNOWSTORM
Each winter, Jerry's cabin became isolated with a large amount of snowfall and his only means to get to Glacier was to walk to the Mt. Baker Highway and catch a ride. (G. Byeman)

refrigerator, he answered, "Ok." Jerry gathered up a few pots and headed for the front door.

The two walked down the drive, crossed the forest service road, and down a path to the river. There was a small steel cable that led out into the water and back again   It reminded Stu of his mother's clothes line but at one point it was under the water. He looked at me and said, "Crank her in." Before long a container surfaced and Stu brought it up the riverbank. It was a water-tight aluminum can. He popped the lid off and put the food inside. Jerry sent it back to the middle, under the cold mountain water.

"Hey," Jerry said," let me tell you a little story about this here spot in the river. When the big shots from

Hollywood were making the movie, 'Call of the Wild,' some of the scenes were shot right here. They had two Indian canoes that were to be floating down this here stretch of river. They put the canoes, loaded with painted-up make-believe Indians with guns and bows and arrows in the river. Then they took off downstream not realizing the rate of the flow and they lost control. They both ended up in that there log jam and both overturned. It was amazing that none of them Indians didn't drown. All the guns went to the bottom of the river and for years, on low water, I would fish them out. Oh, of course they were play guns; no damn good at all."

After walking back to the cabin Jerry asked, "How about some stew? I've

THE FRONT VIEW OF JERRY'S CABIN
The windows at the two levels looked directly at the north face of Mt. Shuksan.
(G. Byeman)

JERRY'S VIEW OF MT. SHUKSAN OUT THE FRONT WINDOW
This view is completely blocked by a new stand of timber today. (G. Byeman)

been cooking it for a few days, Kid."

Stu replied, "Yes, please my name is Stu."

Jerry added, "I like Kid better." He cleared off a spot on the table and pulled up a third hand chair. He then dished up the hot stew and poured more coffee.

After starting to eat, Stu was pleased, surprised at how good it tasted. He asked, "What is in this here great tasting stew, Jerry?"

"Well you start with your onions, spuds, more onions, lots of salt and pepper, water, and meat. In this here I've got white deer (mountain goat) and I think I threw in a grouse or two. I don't remember, I may have thrown in a road kill possum too. Now, the secret is to cook it for days adding some type

of meat—a young bear is good and of course deer."

Stu sat there eating, enjoying the food, and thinking to himself, "Did it really have possum meat in it?"

Upon finishing up, Jerry offered, "How about me showing you around the place?"

Stu jumped up, being ready to see it all. Jerry led the way around the side of the cabin and then to a water wheel which was turning.

Jerry began, "What I miss most up here is being able to listen to the radio. I wanted to hear those news fellows so I rigged up this setup. The water comes out of my pond—some call it Jerry's Lake—but I don't think it's large enough to be called a lake. Now

ONE OF MANY LITTERS OF PUPS THAT JERRY HAD AT THE CABIN
(G. Byeman)

JERRY'S INDIVIDUAL DOG HOUSES
Each dog had a separate chain. The chains were such that the dogs couldn't fight with their neighbor. (G. Byeman)

JERRY BOURN IN FRONT OF HIS GARDEN
(J. Steiner)

JERRY BOURN GETTING READY FOR SOME HUNTING
(R. Krammer)

this wheel turns these sleeves that are connected by belts which then turns the car generator. The juice charges up the truck battery and then I listen to a car radio. I get a few stations in the cabin, mostly Canadian. Now the one program that I must hear each week, I go about fifty feet above the cabin and I then sit outside to listen. Good show, it's worth it.

"You can see that I dammed up the flow out of the pond using my friend, Leck Bottiger's, Cat and some available logs. All these logs are available here because they are on my claims. These are claims that I took over from my old friend Charlie Anderson. As you can see, it is a fairly good-sized pond. I go down around Glacier and catch a bunch of rainbows in the River. I then plant them here. Now this here pond is mine because No. 4 claim crosses this lower end. I have had problems with people thinking they have the right to fish in my pond and I had to straighten that out.

"One time I heard voices and walked up to where we are now. Well, I told them 'You bastards better get the hell out of here. This here is my pond!' Then they headed down to the ranger station and were told that they had the right to fish. Well, you can imagine how this pissed me off on their return. I went to the cabin got the 30-30 and returned. Do you know what a sound shot is? Well, I put one in the pond on each side of them. They high tailed it down the road.

"I knew that I would have some company and within a couple of hours here comes the damn forest service guy and the Whatcom County Sheriff.

JERRY BOURN IN THE CABIN AS AN OLDER MAN
(G. Byeman)

JERRY BOURN'S WATER WHEEL IN THE MIDDLE OF WINTER
This waterwheel provided electrical power to car batteries thus giving Jerry the ability to listen to a car radio. He only got one or two stations part of the time. (G. Byeman)

Well, I was sitting out by the front door with the 30-30 nearby. We could not seem to see eye-to-eye on the matter but they made it very clear not to do it again. I stated that the same thing would happen again. They got up and left; however, that damn ranger didn't give any other fisherman that advice."

Jerry began another story, "Kid, I almost forgot another problem with my good friends at the forest service. A few years ago, the forest service in all of their wisdom, decided to construct a small campground on the high ground at the north side of the pond. Now I was gone working the claim on the creek and when I returned, by damn, here was a nice family camping there. The kids were swimming in the water and fishing boats were out in the middle catching

138

JERRY BOURN'S PRIVATE FISHING POND
Jerry, with the use of a bulldozer, dammed up this area and created his own
fish pond. After his death the logs that made up the dam deteriorated and now
the area is nothing but a marshy area. (G. Byeman)

my fish. I couldn't take this, them being my fish and because part of the pond was on one of my mining claims.

"The dam that I showed you is down by the cabin, so after dark I went out and pulled out the entire stop log dam. Next day, early in the morning, I went to take a look and the whole pond was nothing but a large mud puddle. Before long I could see the campers breaking camp and pulling out. Within two hours, here comes the forest service—it took three of them to make the house call. They started in raving about the mud puddle and how could I do this. Well, I told them, I have the right because of my mining claims and, second, that I had to run the generator because I needed the power.

"Now, the way I fish this here pond was I would watch how big the fish were getting, and when I figured they were a good size, I pull out most of the stop logs in the dam. Those fish would assume that it was their time to go and down over the spillway into my field in front of the cabin they would go. Then I would gather them and have trout for a week or so. You can imagine I got a few visits and warnings from the game department boys. I do the whole procedure a couple of times a year."

As the two of them made their way back to the cabin, Stu was dumbfounded when he saw a horse standing over by a large cedar stump with a cedar roof over it. Stu said excitedly, "Hey, there's your horse, Tony!"

Jerry responded, "Best damn horse that I have ever had. Tony, the one-eyed horse. I got him in a business trade with Doug Hamilton—he got an old truck and I got Tony. Well, when I found he had only one good eye, I thought that

he would be no damn good. But I was wrong. When I take the dogs and him up in the mountains, he is like one of the dogs. He follows me like a dog— no need to tie him up, he just hangs around." Jerry rubbed Tony's nose as they headed back to the cabin.

Stu looked at his watch and said, "I better get back to the highway to catch old Six-Pack Ernie. He should be out of beer and ready to reload in Glacier."

Jerry answered, "Ya, I better feed these animals. Hey Kid, I want to give you this here rock. Look right here. You can see the specks of gold. This here came from the Jack."

Stu looked it over and thanked him a half a dozen times and added, "Jerry, I sure would like to go to a mine with you, but first I'll talk to my mother about it," then he headed down the road.

After returning to Glacier, Stu went to work at Graham's. His mind, however, was miles away thinking about his new buddy, Jerry. His mother returned two days later and Stu could not hold back. He couldn't help but tell her of his visit with Jerry. He confessed, "Mom, I skipped school on Monday. I bet you can't imagine what I did. I went to Jerry Bourn's cabin and spent the whole day there."

Liz's mouth dropped open and there was a look of disbelief in her eyes. She raised her voice, which was something she never did. "You did what? Are you crazy—that man is a wild man! You have seen him many times in town here, and I see how he acts in a drunken rage! You skipped school to go see that crazy man?

"Well, how many times have you skipped school?"

"Only this one time, I swear!" Stu

TONY–JERRY BOURN'S ONE-EYED HORSE
Jerry traded a small truck for Tony. He didn't know at the time of making the deal that Tony was blind in one eye. (G. Byeman)

reassured his mother.

"Please Stuart, tell me why in the world you would do this?" she asked. Stu knew that she was upset especially since she called him by his full name. He was in a world of trouble.

He explained, "Well, I have been talking to Earl about the history of Glacier and the old characters. The subject of Jerry came up, so he gave me a complete history. He says that Jerry is very intelligent—a well-read man. In

spending a few hours with him, I found Earl to be correct. His cabin is full of reading material and he has a car radio that he used to listen to the news and talk programs. He has built all different types of devices up at his cabin."

His mother looked at him and then spoke, "Did Earl tell you that Jerry killed a man in a fight? It happened a few years ago, and they were both in a drunken stupor. He hit him over the head with a rifle butt."

JERRY'S PACK OF DOGS AND TONY WITH THE NORTH FACE OF MT. SHUKSAN IN THE BACKGROUND (G. Byeman)

Stu looked at his mother with a blank look in his eyes. His first thought was Jerry's wife's skull hanging on the cabin. He didn't say what he was thinking—"Holy Shit!"

Stu and his mother didn't speak much the rest of the night. The next day his mother searched for Earl, because she wanted to have a discussion with him about Jerry Bourn. As they sat at a back table during a slow time, she asked, "Earl, you possibly heard that Stu skipped school and spent the day up at Jerry Bourn's cabin. This is the first time that Stu has done a thing like this, and to go to Jerry Bourn's is unthinkable! Please give me your opinion of Jerry. Did he murder a man? When Jerry comes to town he is the worst person I know. How can I allow my son to associate with him?"

"You are right," Earl agreed. "The Jerry that you see here in Glacier is the bottom of the barrel. When he gets his hands on any kind of alcohol here in town or if somebody brings it to his cabin, he is a terrible drunk. I think that the forest service allows him to live up there to keep him away from the rest of society, which I agree with," stated Earl.

"A couple years ago a deputy sheriff stopped in on his way back to town after trying to locate Jerry since he had a warrant for his arrest. We had quite a discussion that day concerning Jerry, and he showed me Jerry's rap sheet over the last 10 or 15 years.

"In that period of time, Jerry had been arrested over 15 times by Whatcom County, and had served over 555 days in the county jail. The charges that were on the rap sheet varied from fighting, drunkenness, driving without a driver's license, lack of insurance, and almost anything else you could imagine. In that discussion, I told the deputy sheriff that I felt that the best place for Jerry was to leave him alone up at

142

Shuksan for he would cause far less trouble there than any other place that he might be. The only time that Jerry really gets in trouble is when he leaves that homestead site up at Shuksan. Finally the deputy agreed with me and said that he would do what he could to leave him alone.

"Another thing about Jerry getting thrown in jail in the wintertime was the fact that he had a much easier life in the compounds of the jail compared to 12 to 15 feet of snow and ice at his cabin site. He had all the food and comforts of a modern home in jail, and I've been told that he was a model prisoner.

"Jerry Bourn, away from drink, is a totally different person. He is a very intelligent man. He is well-read, reading anything of quality he can get his hands on. I save all the magazines

JERRY BOURN READING THE FIRST DEGREE CHARGES AGAINST HIM (Jack Carver Photo-Whatcom Museum, Bellingham, WA)

and newspapers from our home for him. He has an amazing ability to create mechanical machines and can fix anything. When he is sober and at the cabin, he is very respectful of others, particularly of women and kids. His knowledge of wildlife and nature is unbelievable.

"When my two boys were Stu's age, they spent a lot of time with Jerry. I always drove them up, and I would see if Jerry was sober before they could stay. Both of them went mining with him and their knowledge of the outdoors was something I could not have given them."

Liz asked, "Earl, you stated that Jerry was a good fellow when he is sober, right? Well is he really a good fellow or is it that when he is drunk, he such a low life fellow?"

"Truthfully, I think you're right on both counts," Earl answered. With that, the conversation was over.

A few days later, the McKenzies had a discussion about the matter of going to the mine. Liz responded, "Yes, you can go for one day and then we will see."

"Well, thanks Mom but that won't work. It is a long way in and we would be gone for a week or more." The two talked further and Liz agreed that he could go.

Stu waited anxiously for Jerry's next trip into town. That was the only way they could communicate. Within a few days, Jerry popped into town. Seeing Stu, he asked, "Well, I'm heading up. You going to help or not?"

Eagerly Stu replied, "Yes, when do we go?"

"You bring some clothes for a week, rain coat, sleeping bag, and any food you can steal from old Earl here, and be to the cabin on Monday morning. I'm going to pick up grub and then I'm going in for a little drink," Jerry said as he walked away and into Graham's.

They parted about noon and Stu saw him again around six o'clock when he came staggering out of the door of Graham's. Jerry saw Stu, shook his head in embarrassment, and started walking home. Stu wondered, "Would Jerry even remember the proposed trip to the mountain? As he looked over his shoulder, he whispered, "God, I hope my mother didn't see him."

As Stu stood on the boardwalk with his mother waiting for Six-Pack Ernie to show up, Earl came out with a box of groceries. "Here! You two mountain men may need a little grub. Oh, I know you can always live off the land. Another thing—use the common sense that God gave you. No stupid mistakes, Ok?" Earl barked going back into the store. Ernie stopped right on schedule for his first six pack of the day and Stu had his ride.

When Ernie and Stu arrived at the Hannegan Pass Road, Stu realized that with everything he had too much to carry with his gear and box of grub. Ernie said, "I'll take you to the cabin, but if Jerry asks if I have any beer, the answer is 'No.' "

As expected, as soon as Jerry saw whose truck it was, he came a running. "How about a beer Six-Pack?" Jerry questioned.

Ernie answered, "No, I'm on the wagon the start of the week. Sorry." And with that, he left.

All the dogs excitedly jumped around Jerry, each with his or her pack on. Stu noted that Jerry had made a canvas pack for each dog with their name on

it. The names had been painted on with a wide brush. The dogs were eager to go, and Jerry couldn't get them to quit jumping. He repeatedly shouted at them to shut up. Shuksan kept growling at Stu, so Jerry grabbed a piece of rubber hose and wacked him over his butt. The leader of the pack was Lady. The others were Champ, Shuksan, Grizzly, and Thunder. All of the packs were loaded before being placed on the dogs' back. Standing quietly nearby was the one-eyed horse, Tony. Stu noted that all the gear was packed very professionally but he prayed that there was no booze in any of those packs. Jerry placed Stu's gear and food on Tony and the trip began.

"I want you to walk ahead of me today, cause one of these damn dogs might try to take a bite out of you until they get to know you," Jerry remarked.

Stu thought to himself, "Holy god, what did I get myself into?"

Jerry told him to head out to the highway and turn up the Twin Lakes Road. Up that road, they first encountered a crew of loggers doing some Cat logging. Further up, a crew of forest service men were working on the road.

The pace up the road was steady. Stu looked back and saw the dogs were behind Jerry running in and out of the timber. After about four miles, the forest started to give way to open meadows with very steep hillsides. Swamp Creek was raging full with snow melt. Soon, Stu saw a trail veering off to the left and uphill with a beat-up sign, "Gold Run Pass-Gargett Mine."

"Hey Kid, how about getting into some of those cookies you stole from old Earl? How are chances of throwing

JERRY WITH ONE OF THE DOGS WITH HIS HOMEMADE PACK
Jerry on the hillside looking down into the Silesia Creek Valley. Jerry knew
these mountains better than any living man. (G. Byeman)

me a few? Throw straight or the dogs will fight over them. When you are eating yours, turn your back so they can't see what you are doing. Don't worry, in a couple of days they will be your good friends." Jerry assured Stu.

Stu did as directed and then said to Jerry, "Tell me about this here sign and the mine."

"Well," started Jerry, "the Gargett Mine was one of the first in the district being discovered around 1900. Peter Sarr, with a group of boys from Sumas, was the first to find it. A very rich vein, high on Red Mountain, was the point of discovery. I've been to the discovery point a couple of times. The location scared the shit out of me. The boys moved way down the south face and drove an adit into the mountain and made their camp nearby. The mine was originally named the Gold Run Mine but later when the Gargett Family took it over, it became known as the Gargett Mine. The Gargett Brothers have worked in that hole each summer for over 30 years searching for that vein in the Red Mountain. Their adit goes many thousands of feet in the mountain and curves all over. There are many original homestead farms in the Sumas area that were put up as collateral to gain some shares in the mine and as of this date no gold or silver has been found. If they walk away from the claim, I'll file on it and find that damn gold. Let's get the hell going before we fall asleep."

The group started out again with the dogs in the back with Jerry. The Twin Lakes Trail started to steadily climb up out of the Swamp Creek Valley on the north side. After traveling a mile or more Stu saw a building on the other side of Swamp Creek with a trail branching off to it. Again the party stopped, and Stu asked, "Ok, Jerry, what is this one?"

"This here is the Evergreen Mine," Jerry remarked, "and up over that there ridge is the Blonden Mine. The Evergreen was a lead mine to serve the war effort and the Blonden was much earlier. It was a gold claim. The lead turned out to be very low grade, not suitable for bullets and there wasn't much gold up high. The Evergreen is owned by a fellow in Chicago and I don't know who has ownership of the gold mine. Oh, up there where the creek turns there was a tent village at the time of discovery in 1897. Union City was its name. Let's get going."

The trail continued to climb with views of all the high mountains and the valley floors. The trail turned a corner and Stu could not believe the beauty of the two alpine lakes in front. Jerry joined Stu. The pack of dogs ran past them like they were shot out of a gun. Jerry explained, "Kid, these here are the Twin Lakes that old Jack Post discovered in 1897 and named. He named that there mountain Winchester Mountain. The forest service boys built a fire lookout on top a few years back. The dogs are your friends by now I think."

Suddenly Jerry and Stu could hear sound of barking coming from between the lakes. Jerry grabbed the 30-30 off Tony's pack and started running ahead. When the two got to the level spot between the lakes, they saw a camp and two guys out on the lake in a manmade raft. Jerry said, "Oh shit, I was hoping the dogs had a bear up a tree and we could get fresh meat. We better go over

**ONE OF THE OLD TIMERS, BERT LOWRY,
AT TWIN LAKES IN THE EARLY 1900'S
(C. Kvistad)**

TWO MAN RAFT ON UPPER TWIN LAKE
This raft was constructed from floating trees around the lake. How does this
look safe when you realize that the water temperature is only a few degrees
above freezing? (P. Maiers)

TWIN LAKES–ELEVATION 5200 FEET
(G. Byeman)

UPPER TWIN LAKE
(M. Impero)

and tie those damn dogs to those trees or they will help themselves to those fellow's camp and tear it to hell."

The two men came ashore and Stu could see Jerry looking into the edge of the lake to see if they had some beer or wine, but Stu was in luck again, as these two were part of a church group hiking the Cascades. After a short conversation about the weather, flies and bugs, fishing, and the beauty of the lakes, the two went on their way.

On the move again, Jerry told Stu that they had reached the high point for the day and now they would be going downhill. The party skirted around the upper lake on the original Lone Jack Trail that had been well constructed but not wide enough for a wagon. Stu realized that everything that came in, had to come by pack animals. He asked Jerry about freighting and pack animals.

Jerry answered, "Don't know much about the first two operations at the Lone Jack. They were before Charlie Bourn's days."

As the party went through Twin Lakes Pass, Stu saw a third lake, much smaller than the other two. Within minutes, he saw the working of another mine and he remembered, from what someone in Glacier told him, that this was the Saginaw Workings. "Jerry," inquired Stu, "What is the story of the Saginaw Mine here?" Jerry kept walking, "It was discovered about the time of the Jack and to date has had many owners. It's gold and silver. Right now, Bob Averill of Bellingham is the owner. He owns a jewelry store in Bellingham. Nice guy. He stops in at the cabin all the time and brings some beer or wine. Say Kid, when you were stealing the food from old Earl, why

didn't you get us some alcohol?"

Jerry told him that now they were on the High Trail to the Lone Jack. This trail was put in for empty pack trains to come out. Jerry explained that in the heyday of the Brooks/Willis Operation, his dad, Charlie Bourn, could have up to two pack trains a day coming and going; a total of fifty horses or mules. The trail remained level and suddenly the view of Lulu Gulch and the Brooks/Willis bunkhouse, the only remaining building standing, came into view.

The two descended crossing Lulu Creek and they finally came to the old bunkhouse. Stu was ready to call it a day. After stopping at the door, less door frame and door, Jerry paused then said, "Well Kid, she isn't the Hilton Hotel but if it rains it will keep our sorry asses dry along with at least a hundred pack rats." The next hour they spent unloading

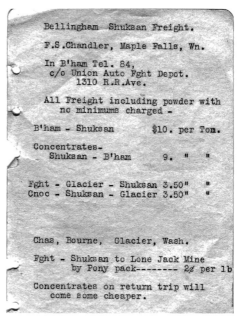

Bellingham Shuksan Freight.

F.S.Chandler, Maple Falls, Wn.

In B'ham Tel. 84,
c/o Union Auto Fght Depot.
1310 R.R.Ave.

All Freight including powder with
no minimums charged -

B'ham - Shuksan $10. per Ton.

Concentrates-
Shuksan - B'ham   9. "   "

Fght - Glacier - Shuksan 3.50" "
Cnoc - Shuksan - Glacier 3.50" "

Chas, Bourne, Glacier, Wash.

Fght - Shuksan to Lone Jack Mine
by Pony pack-------- 2¢ per lb

Concentrates on return trip will
come some cheaper.

BELLINGHAM-SHUKSAN FREIGHT–CHAS BOURN FREIGHT RATES
(J. Munroe)

LONE JACK TRAIL ABOVE THE THIRD LAKE–WINCHESTER LAKE
Winchester Lake was named by Jack Post, discoverer of the Lone Jack gold mine. (J. Munroe)

LONE JACK HIGH TRAIL DROPPING INTO LULU GLUCH
The whole area around the Lone Jack burned from a large forest fire following the fire that destroyed the Jack in 1906. (D. Palmer)

**SECTION OF LONE JACK TRAIL FOLLOWING
THE DEVASTATING FOREST FIRE**
This hillside looked this way for years to come. (J. Munroe)

all the packs from the horse and the dogs. Jerry checked each animal for back sores and sore feet, and then they, including Tony, were off to try to find something to eat.

Jerry and Stu carried almost everything personal inside and laid it out in piles. "At some point in time, there may have been some type of furnishings and flooring in here, but now, as you can see, there is nothing but three level tiers of ground. We have running water. See that pipe over there? And we have a steady flow of water. Now you didn't expect running hot water did you? We'll get one of the gas lights going and we will be able to see something."

Next, Jerry showed Stu how to hang all the food bags from the roof rafters. They set up everything for cooking outdoors and cut tree branches to place under their sleeping bags. Finally, they got the fire started and put the coffee pot in place.

Jerry said that they would be eating a can of beans with some ham. After dinner, Stu noticed that Jerry had not fed the dogs, and he became worried. Old Tony was busy eating leaves off alder and blueberry brushes. Finally Stu could not take it any longer and asked Jerry, "What about food for the dogs?"

Jerry answered "Later."

The sunset behind Bear Mountain was very early at this time of year, and the two sat drinking coffee looking at the colors across Silesia Creek on the Skagit Range. They could see the highest point, Post Mountain.

Jerry went to one of Tony's packs and came out with a 22 pistol.

Stu said, "For bears or what?"

Jerry remarked, "Dog food."

As darkness approached, the two went inside. Jerry told the dogs to get the hell outside. After adding a second light, they built a bench, attached it to a side wall, and the two settled on the bench and waited.

Soon Stu could see little beady eyes looking at them from the hidden corners of the underside of the roof. Jerry took aim with the 22, hit the trigger, and one of the monsters fell to the floor. He took aim again and the second pack rat hit the deck. Jerry said, "These are nice fat ones this summer. We will figure two per dog for dinner. Kid, you pop a couple. We'll stop at about ten for the dogs. We don't want to over shoot them. We need breeding stock for next year."

Stu took aim and missed. Three times in a row he missed. The pack rats got braver and closer. Jerry murmured, "Kid, if you don't hit one soon, we will run out of bullets, or they'll be eating out of your hand."

On the fourth shot, Stu killed one. After counting out ten rats, Jerry said, "Well, let's gather them up. Whatever you do don't hand feed anything to one of these dogs. They may take your hand off at your wrist. I will go and tie each one with a short rope to trees and then the feeding can begin."

When Jerry returned, Stu asked, "Do we need to gut them or something?" Jerry didn't bother to answer and gathered the rats in a bag. He dropped two rats per dog. Stu could see why it would not be wise to get near them when they were eating. Two bites per rat were normal.

Jerry announced, "Let's turn in."

Stu woke to a gunshot the following morning. He sat up with a start and could hear the pack rats stirring, due

**JERRY AND STU'S HOME FOR TWO WEEKS AT THE
BROOKS/WILLIS MINE BUNKHOUSE
(B. Peters)**

to the shot. He turned to look over at Jerry and noted that his sleeping bag was empty. There was no trace of him outside so Stu got the coffee pot going on the fire that Jerry had rebuilt. In about forty-five minutes, Jerry came back from the direction of Garrison Creek. In one hand was the 30-30 and in the other he held something over his shoulder.

As he neared, Stu could see that it was the hind quarter of a deer. His mouth dropped open. Jerry said, "Get a short piece of rope and we will hang it here in the portal of the Lulu Shaft. There is a nice flat meadow over there that's a great place for hunting. Each year I get a nice young deer. Now we got some wonderful eatens." Stu then realized Jerry hadn't bothered to take much meat along because he knew

that those deer would be there. Stu also knew that deer season didn't open for two more months. Apparently that didn't seem to hinder Jerry.

While they were finishing their breakfast of bread and venison steaks, Jerry commented on the plan for the day, "This morning we will head up the Lone Jack Vein which was the point of discovery of the whole thing. I'm hoping that this year the snow has melted back further than normal and that will expose a section of the vein that I have worked before. We'll take rock hammers and some bags for gathering up the rock. The dogs can haul the ore down to here. Tony will stay here. It's too steep for him."

The trail was hard to follow at some points due to the fact that it crossed an avalanche chute, but Jerry, if he got off

**BROOKS/WILLIS ORE MILL BUILDING WITH THREE-TIER
BUNKHOUSE ABOVE
(J. Munroe)**

it for a minute, could easily get back on it. Again Jerry told Stu the story of the Mt. Baker Mining Company. Their ore mill was down near Silesia Creek. A tramway carried the ore from high on this hillside to the mill. The tram would have been at this point directly overhead, 120 feet high. Breaking over a small ridge, they came into an open basin. High on the hillside Jerry pointed to the location that they were heading. They continued up the old trail and at a certain point Jerry said, "Time to head straight up."

Stu looked in disbelief and quickly replied, "Jerry that is too steep for me. I will fall and kill myself!"

Jerry reasoned, "No, no you will be fine. The dogs go up there all the time."

Thirty minutes later, the two men and five dogs were all standing on the ledge. Stu held on and didn't look down. Jerry said disgustedly, "Damn it all! The snow hasn't melted more than normal. Damn it all! See this here in the vein, that there is quartz; the plan was to go south, but the damn snow has not melted. Damn."

While it was bad news for Jerry, Stu thought to himself, "Well, now we can get down from this spot!" He started looking for hand holes to climb down

BROOKS /WILLIS BUNKHOUSE ON MAY 15, 1925
(J. Munroe)

RUSTING EQUIPMENT FROM THE BROOKS/WILLIS ORE MILL
(T. Anderson)

but Jerry said, "Well, now that we are here, let's work on this section of vein today."

Stu looked over his shoulder and whispered to himself, "Ok, Jerry, I'm going to die today."

The two worked the bulk of the day with Jerry chipping off quartz rock, and Stu gathering them and placing them in the dog's pack bags. When Jerry found special rocks, he would stop and show Stu the flecks of gold. Small as they were you could sure see the gold. As the day worn on, Stu realized that they had not taken a lunch or even taken the time for a drink of water.

Perched on that ledge and scared to death, Stu's mouth was dirt dry. He could hike down to one of the cascading water streams below, but he knew that

if he went down there would be no returning.

After a few hours of work, Jerry decided it was time to forget it. "I truly think that if I could get under that snow field, good gold is there for the taking. We'll load up the dog packs, gather the tools, and head down to camp," Jerry said somewhat disappointed. The two headed down, with Stu requesting to go last. He turned around facing in, and climbed down very cautiously. Twenty minutes later he reached flat ground and turned around. Jerry was a good two hundred yards ahead whistling away and the dogs were already out of sight heading down to camp for another great dinner.

Back at camp, after unloading the dog packs, Jerry located a piece of cast iron, shaped like a bowl that he had stored under an uprooted stump. With a hammer he set to work breaking up the ore from the Jack. Jerry showed Stu how to crush the rock and Jerry set out panning the fines. After a few hours and little gold to show for their work, Jerry barked, "Well shit, this is next to nothing, not worth our time.

"Tomorrow, we will go into the Lulu shaft and work over a roof pillar. A roof pillar is made from solid rock, supporting the inside of the stope ceiling. The stope is the mining room area of the mine. These big shot mining engineers and safety people feel they are needed for safety. They are wrong; don't need them. This here rock is the most solid in the world. I've been taking out these pillars for years and she

hasn't fell down yet."

Stu sat a few moments and then asked, "Jerry, who owns this land and this mine?"

"Well, "Jerry started out slowly, "This here is owned by a man in Bellingham by the name of Harry Bullene. Harry is a good friend of mine. He says it is ok for me to do a little digging around. He thinks of me as kind of the guard and caretaker of the property." Stu turned away and smiled to himself.

Their dinner was the same as the previous night, except that it was beans and venison steaks. The dogs had pack rats. The next morning, the two headed into the Lulu portal with hammers and bags to carry the rock. Jerry had hidden some carbide lamps under the corner

LONE JACK VEIN THAT JERRY AND STU WORKED ON
(M. Impero)

of a rock and with these they had lights for the day. They dressed with an extra layer for warmth due to the cold air within the mountain. The shaft went in on a sweeping turn with secondary adits going off many different directions.

Jerry said, "Hey Kid, I want to show you something in this back corner."

Turning the corner, they came to a room full of dynamite boxes. Stu's mouth fell open, and he questioned very softly as if the sound would set it off, "Jerry, is this what I think it is, dynamite? Is it dangerous and will it explode?" Jerry went forward and sat down on a box.

Jerry took his hammer and started pounding on another box. "No, I don't think she will blow at all. Been here too long. See that jelly type stuff there on the floor? That there is nitro draining out of the powder. When it is gone, she becomes an awful low grade. Not a good thing to drink water in the Lulu. This here powder has been here since the failure of the Brooks/Willis operation. Yes, old Harry knows it is here, but it's not doing any harm. Oh, hell, let's take a break," Jerry hollered as he sat down on one of the lower boxes and started to roll a cigarette. Stu sat in disbelief and said nothing. Jerry then lit her up and smoked it. Stu didn't say a word for an hour.

Stu and Jerry walked to the end of the shaft and found the years-old wood ladder. They climbed up about sixty feet to a big open area which Jerry had told him was called a stope. The floor was sloping, and the height of the room represented the height of the vein. Stu saw that in the middle of this particular room was one of the rock pillars that Jerry had told him about. Stu stopped

and took a serious look. These pillars had been left to provide safety for the miners, and now he and Jerry were planning to remove this one. His mother would have a fit!

The two unlikely partners went back out and carried in Jerry's cast iron bowl and the gold pan. They chipped, crushed, and panned for three days. Jerry's little container for gold started to fill and each night there was talk about what the next day would bring.

On the third day, Jerry growing tired of the Lulu said, "What you say, Kid, if we head out tomorrow and stop there at the Sileisa Creek Trail? We'll hike down to do some sluicing in the creek."

Stu thought to himself, "Why not? Don't have a clue what sluicing is, but ok."

The two were sitting around the campfire after having another venison dinner. Stu had become a good friend to Jerry's dog, Grizzly. He was petting Grizzly's head as he had laid down next to him. Jerry commented, "I may have to give you old Grizzly there. You and him are becoming such good buddies."

Stu thought to himself, "Oh, sure, I'd take old Grizzly to school with me and watch him eat a couple of kids."

"Jerry," Stu questioned, "you told me about the tramway and the location of the first mill but how about more information on that first operation?"

"Well" started Jerry, "a good old boy by the name of Jack Post first discovered gold up here on Bear Mountain in the summer of 1897. Jack was a true sourdough mountain man. Some say that I'm a mountain man like Jack. I think it's damn good to be in the same league as Jack.

"Jack, with two other fellows from

158

**DYNAMITE STORAGE ROOM IN THE LULU TUNNEL
OF THE LONE JACK**
(D. Palmer)

Sumas, were camped at Twin Lakes when the discovery was made. Jack had a wife and family in Sumas, but they were secondary to his prospecting. He worked the creeks and hillsides here and across the border in Canada. The three were smart and did the right thing. Within four months they sold it to a company from Portland. and the Portland people formed the Mt. Baker Mining Company.

"This discovery started the Mt. Baker Gold Rush and was a major factor in the organization of the Mt. Baker Mining District. Now, these Portland boys had no idea where the Lone Jack was. They were not aware of the roughest of the Cascade Mountains, the amount of winter-time snow, nor the remoteness of the region. In 1897, there wasn't even a wagon road to Glacier and the Nooksack had to be forded down by Jake Steiner's place. No railroad closer than Sumas. The area was totally a wilderness. The main trail was the Swamp Creek—same way as we came and the other was up Silesia Creek from Canada.

"The Mt. Baker Mining Co. sold mining stock throughout the northwest with local people jumping on the band wagon. The company's main office remained in Portland, and they were closed mouth about the operation. This secret method, before long, upset the local folks but the lack of communications continued. They boasted early on that the mine would be producing gold by the end of 1898. This turned to be so far off that again the shareholders began to question what was going on.

"With the arrival of the Bellingham Bay and British Columbia Railroad to Maple Falls, this was the break that was needed to get the ball rolling. With the railroad, the roads and trails of the valley started to develop rapidly.

"I will give these boys credit,"Jerry continued, "they were somewhat smarter when it came to laying out a mining operation in a wild area. Now, the fools of the Brooks-Willis operation were a whole different matter. They laid out all the buildings right in the path of a yearly avalanche. The Mt. Baker Boys moved all the supplies and machinery up the Swamp Creek Valley and then down Lulu Gulch. Right behind you there, they constructed the mill and living quarters down in the trees, out of avalanche danger. They ran an overhead tramway from there up to the Lone Jack Vein where we were a few days ago.

"I think it was in August of 1903 that the first cleanup of gold at the Lone Jack was made. For the next few years, they averaged about $30,000 per month, which was a hell of a lot of money in those days. Finally in 1904, the secret company in Portland paid a dividend and the local folks saw a future and expected the same thing three to four times a year. Well, it didn't happen. The hard feelings started to build again. At about this time, the Lone Jack Vein was petering out and they moved the tram down to the Lulu and started mining that ore.

"In the summer of 1907, a fire started in the Lone Jack Mill building and completely destroyed the whole thing. The total mill building and bunkhouses/cookhouse were gone. Oh yes, there was one building, a bunkhouse that survived. It stood until a few years ago. It created a major forest fire that

160

**GOLD-BEARING QUARTZ ROCK SUPPORTING THE
CEILING OF THE LULU**
**The vein is between six to eight feet wide and the pillar is four to five feet in
diameter. (M. Impero)**

burned almost to Twin Lakes. You could see the effects of that fire years later. See over there? The cause of the fire was said to have started in the mill building, however some feel the cause was manmade. Some of local folk were getting real upset with the boys in Portland so rumor has it that they hiked in and started the fire. I think that there is a hell of lot of gold remaining right there in old Bear Mountain.

"Big Andy Ecklund was the real man of the Lone Jack. He was living in Bellingham, and he would come by my place a few times a year. He started working up here in the construction of the whole damn thing and worked until the fire. He was not a big man at all but because of the respect that the others gave him, he was known as 'Big Andy' by all. Andy became the man for the boys in Portland and ended up doing all types of jobs.

"Andy got word that a new cook and his Indian wife were to arrive in Glacier, and he was to hike down and guide them to the Jack. Andy walked to Glacier and met the train. There he met the man and an Indian woman, who introduced themselves and then the shock came when Andy saw a four-year-old boy. A sickly boy at that, standing next to them. Andy said to himself, 'I think the man and wife can make it, but what about this kid?' Andy thought and came up with a solution.

161

**LULU STOPE AREA WITH WOOD PILLARS
INSTEAD OF ROCK PILLARS**
One of Jerry's dogs came inside for a little rest. (J. Christenson)

He found a gunny sack in a store. He picked up the kid, put him in the sack, threw him over his shoulder, and walked back to the Jack with the boy's parents. This family stayed there over one winter and then headed out. By the time they left the kid was doing fine-'mountain air.'

"One time, Andy cut four fingers off his hand, wrapped them up, walked to Glacier, caught the train and spent two weeks in a Bellingham hospital.

"There were between twenty-five and thirty men working at the Jack at one point. Following the start of the operation, for the next three or four years, they worked year round. I can't think of a more isolated place on earth with between twenty and thirty feet of snow, which would last from the first of November until the end of June. All food, provisions, and supplies had to be hauled in by November as all freighting stopped in the winter.

"The Cress Brothers were the most interesting young men when they went to work at the Jack. John Cress was sixteen years old when he approached Big Andy in the hospital about a job at the Jack. John had arrived in Bellingham from Colorado. He read about Andy's accident at the Jack and thought that it would be a hell of a fine place to work. Andy took an immediate liking to the young man and hired him on the spot.

"Andy, on his return to the Jack with John, took the train to Glacier and then had to walk. He had taken a look at John's work shoes, and he told him they wouldn't do. John's feet blistered badly on the way in but he didn't say a word to Andy. John took an immediate liking to the Jack and loved the alpine country. If he was lucky, in the early morning or late in the afternoon, he could see black bears or mountain goats. At this time, these animals were few and far between because of the heavy hunting that all the prospectors did.

"John had a variety of jobs, from helping remove the gold from mercury to dumping ore buckets in the ore mill. That first winter he stayed the whole time and did not go out for six months. When he finally went out, he sent a letter to his younger brother, Dave, in Colorado about the great job he had. In a month, Dave arrived and also got a job at the Jack. The two of them handled all types of work, wood cutting to mining in the mountain. One job they both had at different times was hunting for fresh meat—it could be bear, goat, deer, or almost any living thing. The two worked there until the fire and then they moved on.

"Oh, another job that Andy and the two Cress Brothers had was to transport the gold to Bellingham, which included the safeguarding of the gold. With the Jack finally producing gold, a new problem was created for the Mt. Baker Mining Company—that being how to get the pure 30 pounds of gold from the east side of Bear Mountain to a bank with a safe.

"The only method of transporting the gold was on a man's back, as most of the year the trail was snow-covered and horses could not make the trip. The man chosen for this duty again was that man, Big Andy. Big Andy realized that he would need a guard on each trip and he choose the two Cress Brothers for the job.

JACK POST AS A YOUNG MAN OF SUMAS
(J. Munroe)

"Following Andy's suggestion, the company cast the solid gold into bars that were about 1 x 4 x 6 inches. Andy's wife sewed a special vest that he could wear under a normal coat so that it was not seen. He, along with one of the Cress Boys, carried out gold once a month, either on the Twin Lakes Trail or down Silesia Creek into Canada. They had no set pattern or schedule; sometimes in the middle of the night or throughout the day. Andy was the main man who carried the gold, but sometimes it was the other way around. The guard would walk about a hundred yards behind the carrier with no light. They had a system of signals with the light for potential robbery. Over the years, there were numerous attempts by the bad guys to get the gold but these two were never robbed. Well, that's enough. Time for some shut eye."

They found the trail and loaded the sluice box on Tony, along with shovels

163

**JACK POST ON A PROSPECTING AND FISHING TRIP–
BELIEVED TO BE ON SILESIA CREEK
(J. Munroe)**

and picks. The dogs each had an empty pack on their back and down the trail they went. In a couple of hours, Jerry turned off the trail and headed down to the roaring creek. Tony and the dogs made it to the creek before the men. Unloading the box and setting up in the creek took a good hour.

As Stu helped Jerry, he noticed red ribbons on some of the trees and a sign that read, "FEDERAL GOVERNMENT PLACER MINING CLAIM" with two names of men listed below. Stu asked Jerry, "What is this here mining claim? What's Placer Claim? You know these two guys?"

Jerry answered, "Placer mining claim is one where the gold is found

in the creek bed having been washed down from the mountain side. See, we are directly below the Jack. The gold in the Jack is in the solid rock." Jerry didn't answer who the two guys were.

"In the operation of a sluice box, there are three things that must be right for a successful operation. The box must be set at the proper grade, with the right amount of incoming water, and the right selection of gravelly material from the creek bed." It took Jerry about an hour to get it set right and then they operated it again. In no time, they could see gold speckles backing up behind the box ribs. The two partners were now successful.

Suddenly Jerry stopped working and

**BERT LOWRY (left) AND JACK POST STANDING ON BERT'S
ROADHOUSE PORCH IN SHUKSAN
(C. Kvistad)**

listened. Stu could also hear the dogs barking like mad. They could make out men's voices coming down the hillside. Jerry stopped working and ran to the tree that Tony was tied to and untied him. He said to Stu, "Ok, run like hell up the hill. I'll meet you at the Lakes. Go straight up the hill. You can't miss the lakes."

Stu asked, "What the hell is going on Jerry and what about the dogs and Tony?"

Jerry barked, "Haven't got time to talk! The dogs and Tony will meet us there or at the cabin. Now, get the hell going!"

The dogs, Tony, Jerry, and Stu were one hundred yards up the hill when they heard the men who owned the claim shouting, "God damn you, Jerry, we know that it's you. Now stay off our claim or we will shoot your sorry ass!"

Stu ran as hard as he could up the hill hearing the dogs and Tony around him. He fell down at least a half dozen times but got up, and continued up the steep hillside. Soon, he was in dense forest and couldn't hear a thing. He slowed down to a steady climb wondering what the hell that was all about, and in an hour, he was in the meadows around Twin Lakes. He went through the pass and there were three of the five dogs and Tony standing under a big alpine mountain hemlock. Stu sat down and Grizzly came over wanting to be petted.

An hour later, Jerry came into view at the east end of the upper lake with the other two dogs. Soon they were all sitting under the tree and Jerry knew what was coming.

Stu asked, "Well, Jerry, how are chances of you filling me in on the claim?"

"Kid, you see, for years no one posted a claim down there on the creek and I, along with others, were free to work any area we wanted. Well, these damn fools came along and filed on the best spot down there. I knew that it was the best spot but you file on a claim and everyone realizes that it's good. I've been working their claim for years and they can't catch me. Oh, they know it's me, but they can't prove it. And if they could, so what? They'll probably take me to jail."

"Jerry, one last question," asked Stu. "What about the gear—the box and shovels?"

Jerry replied, "Oh, each time I go down there I borrow their equipment."

As they stood up preparing to leave, Jerry took one look at Stu and broke out in an uncontrollable laugh. "My god, look at you! Your shirt and your pants are all torn to hell now and I'm going to start calling you Jack Post, the old mountain man. Now you look like him."

They gathered up their gear, reloaded the dogs, and, then Tony headed down. By the time Stu got to Jerry's cabin, he was exhausted but he knew he better get home. Stu said, "It was a great trip. I had the most fun I've had in my life. Give me a few days and I'll be ready to go again."

Jerry remarked, "I'll figure out how much we got and give you your share. Oh, one thing, Kid, some of the things we did you'll want to keep to yourself."

Stu nodded as he started to walk down the road. Stu waited by the road for a ride and in a matter of minutes a forest service truck gave him the needed ride. The ranger asked, "Stu, what have you been up to in the mountain?"

"Oh, I spent the day with Jerry

Bourn," answered Stu.

The ranger quickly responded, "He is sure a rotten son of a bitch." Stu looked out the window and smiled.

Stu wondered what he was going to tell his mother—first shooting an illegal deer, then working a mine owned by someone else, and finally working a placer claim that belonged to the two men named on the sign. He realized that he better come up with something real quick.

Stu walked from the ranger station down to Graham's and walked through the front door. His mother came charging out from the kitchen and in shock said, "Oh my god look at you! You're dirty, your pants and shirt are torn all to hell and my god, you smell like dogs! Oh my god you didn't get near those dogs, did you? Well, fill me in! How did it go? It looks like you're in one piece."

"All those crazy dogs are my friends now! I don't hand feed them, not yet." Stu said. We worked on the Lone Jack Vein a few days and got a small amount of gold, then we did some digging around the Lulu tunnel and did well. We went down to Silesia Creek and Jerry taught me how to pan for gold. Over all, it was a great trip and I ate real well. Jerry knows what kind of food to bring."

Liz took one more look at her son and said, "Ok, you can tell me more later. Please go take a bath." As Stu walked past Earl at the end of the bar, Earl gave him a big wink.

FAREWELL TO GLACIER

Stu had learned much from his six years in Glacier. He had stories to last a lifetime. The day had come that he was to go to Seattle with his mother to be inducted into the Army.

Stu and his mother sat at the small table in the little cabin and a conversation began. Stu asked, "Mother, now that I'm leaving, I'm concerned about your well-being. What are your future plans?"

His mother looked at him and slowly answered, "Well, Stuart, I am returning to Seattle today as you go into the service. You see, we really didn't lose our house in Seattle and I am returning to it. I've had the house rented out and I've been receiving monthly rental checks. My plan was to bring you up to this godforsaken place and hopefully it would make a man out of you. I do believe that for both of us it was an excellent move, and it certainly made a man out of you." She added, "With the money that I've saved from working here and the sizable amount of money that your father left me, I can now go back to Seattle and live comfortably, or go find myself another great job."

Stu looked at his mother with a look of disbelief and said, "Well mother, you sure bull-shitted me. Oh, sorry, I guess I was around Jerry too much, but I wouldn't have had it any other way."

The following day while loading their bags into the car to go to Seattle, all of a sudden they heard Earl and Mrs. Earl. They wished both of the McKenzies the best possible luck and to Stuart, Earl said, "Keep your head down." At this point, they all shed a few tears.

As Liz and Stu were about to get into the car they turned, and there were five of the Boys standing off to the side in no particular order.

**JERRY HIGH ON THE EAST SIDE OF PLEIADES RIDGE WITH
GRIZZLY
(G. Byeman)**

On the left stood Pamp Bottiger, hand in hand with his son, Frankie, and on the opposite end stood Jerry with a leash on Grizzly. Jerry bent down and untied the leash. Grizzly walked slowly up to Stu. Stu went down to one knee and affectionately petted the dog. In a couple of minutes, Jerry gave a simple command and Grizzly returned to his side.

None of them spoke, however Jumbo stepped forward, planted his heels together, stood very erect and made a very slow, perfect salute. They all turned, with their heads slightly bent, and started to walk back into Graham's.

As they were driving away, Stu turned and looked over his shoulder to say goodbye.